Child Poverty
in Canada

Child Poverty in Canada

Patrizia Albanese

ISSUES IN CANADA

OXFORD
UNIVERSITY PRESS

OXFORD
UNIVERSITY PRESS

8 Sampson Mews, Suite 204, Don Mills, Ontario M3C 0H5
www.oupcanada.com

Oxford University Press is a department of the University of Oxford.
It furthers the University's objective of excellence in research, scholarship,
and education by publishing worldwide in

Oxford New York

Auckland Cape Town Dar es Salaam Hong Kong Karachi Kuala Lumpur Madrid
Melbourne Mexico City Nairobi New Delhi Shanghai Taipei Toronto

With offices in

Argentina Austria Brazil Chile Czech Republic France Greece
Guatemala Hungary Italy Japan Poland Portugal Singapore
South Korea Switzerland Thailand Turkey Ukraine Vietnam

Oxford is a trade mark of Oxford University Press in the UK and in certain other countries

Published in Canada by Oxford University Press

Library and Archives Canada Cataloguing in Publication

Albanese, Patrizia
Child poverty in Canada / Patrizia Albanese.

(Issues in Canada)
Includes bibliographical references and index.
ISBN 978-0-19-543205-3

1. Poor children—Canada. 2. Poverty—Canada. I. Title. II. Series: Issues in Canada.

HV745.A6A43 2009   305.23086'9420971   C2009-904662-8

Cover image: Courtesy of Dick Loek, PhotoSensitive

Oxford University Press is committed to our environment. The book is printed on Forest
Stewardship Council certified paper which contains 100% post-consumer waste.
Printed and bound in Canada.

1 2 3 4 — 13 12 11 10

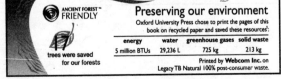

Preserving our environment

Oxford University Press chose to print the pages of this
book on recycled paper and saved these resources[1]:

energy	water	greenhouse gases	solid waste
5 million BTUs	29,236 L	725 kg	213 kg

trees were saved
for our forests

Printed by **Webcom Inc.** on
Legacy TB Natural 100% post-consumer waste.

ANCIENT FOREST™
FRIENDLY

FSC

Mixed Sources
Product group from well-managed
forests, controlled sources and
recycled wood or fiber

Cert no. SW-COC-002358
www.fsc.org
© 1996 Forest Stewardship Council

[1]Estimates were made using the Environmental Defense Paper Calculator.

HV
745
.A6
A43
2010

Contents

List of Illustrations

List of Tables

Abbreviations

BMI	Body Mass Index
CAP	Canada Assistance Place
CBC	Canadian Broadcasting Corporation
CHST	Canada Health and Social Transfer
CMA	Census Metropolitan Area
CMHC	Canada Mortgage and Housing Corporation
CRC (UN CRC)	United Nations Convention on the Rights of the Child
EI	Employment Insurance (formerly UI: Unemployment Insurance)
EQAO	Ontario Education Quality and Accountability Office (Standardized testing)
EU	European Union
GDP	Gross Domestic Product
LICO	Low-Income Cut-Off
LIM	Low-Income Measure
LSIC	Longitudinal Survey of Immigrants to Canada
MBM	Market Basket Measure

NLSCY	National Longitudinal Survey of Children and Youth
OECD	Organization for Economic Co-operation and Development
PPVT-R	Peabody Picture Vocabulary Test–Revised
UN	United Nations
UNICEF	United Nations Children's Fund

Introduction

Canada, the Envy of the World?

Most Canadians believe that their country is prosperous, fair-minded, and respectful of human rights—put simply: the envy of the world. And on some level, there is reason to believe this. In November 2000, national headlines reported "Canada #1 in UN Survey—Again" (CBC News 2000). The CBC, like other news outlets, proudly proclaimed that for the seventh year in a row Canada ranked at the top of the United Nations Human Development Index, part of the annual UN *Human Development Report*. Starting in 1990, the Index ranks the basic living conditions across 174 countries, including life expectancy, adult literacy rates, and standard of living.[1] Using these measures, Canada sat at the top of the Index in 2000 (Albanese 2009b). However, the Index is only a partial measure of human development, and the UN warns that Canada falls surprisingly far behind in areas such as human rights and poverty.

At the same time as the Index's release in 2000, Campaign 2000, a cross-Canada public education movement to build awareness and support for a 1989 all-party House of Commons resolution to end child poverty in Canada by the year 2000, issued its first *Child Poverty in Canada Report Card*.

While Canada celebrated its top position on the UN Human Development Index that year, Campaign 2000 reported that child poverty rates "grew to a record high." At the end of 2000, 1 in 5 children lived in poverty—an increase of 402,000 children since 1989 (Campaign 2000 2000).

The UN's Convention on the Rights of the Child and Canada's obligations

In 1989 the United Nations General Assembly adopted the Convention on the Rights of the Child (CRC). The 54 articles of the CRC include a universally agreed upon set of standards and obligations to protect a child's rights and well-being. The articles are founded on the principles of respect for the dignity and worth of each individual, regardless of race, colour, gender, language, religion, opinions, origins, wealth, birth status, or ability; they are expected to apply to every child around the world. Its four key commitments are: (1) the best interests of the child; (2) survival and development; (3) children's participation; and (4) non-discrimination. Upon ratifying this agreement, governments are obliged to help improve conditions for children everywhere. This document has been negotiated and signed by 192 heads of state, yet remains to be ratified by the United States and Somalia.

By signing the CRC, the Canadian government is committed to recognizing "the right of every child to a standard of living adequate for the child's physical, mental, spiritual, moral and social development" (article 27). The CRC explains that the primary responsibility of a parent or guardian is to secure the necessary living conditions for a child's development, but also specifies that governments should assist parents by implementing support programs that provide nutrition, clothing, and housing. The CRC, along with a number of national and international documents and declarations supported by Canada—including the United Nation's "A World Fit for Children" and Canada's "A Canada Fit for Children"—has established the elimination of child poverty as a policy objective of top priority. However, putting principles into practice has proven to be challenging; despite the CRC's objectives, Canada remains among the least successful at addressing child poverty among modern, industrialized nations.

Is There a Child Poverty "Problem" in Canada?

Many Canadians are surprised to know that Canada ranks poorly compared to other industrialized nations when it comes to child poverty. Some have even denied that we have a child poverty "problem" in this country, arguing that we don't have "real" poverty—that some individuals and families only "feel" poor because they have less than "average" Canadians. But most people would agree that not having enough to eat is a good indication that one is poor—and Food Banks Canada (formerly the Canadian Association of Food Banks) confirms that this is a growing reality for many Canadians.

Food bank use

In March 2008, 704,414 individuals were assisted by a food bank or affiliated food program in Canada. This represents a 6 percent increase since 1997, the first year comparable data were available. According to a national survey of food bank users, food banks in Ontario, Quebec, and British Columbia accounted for 78 percent of food bank use in Canada (See Table I.1). Almost half (42 percent) of food banks in Canada saw an increase in the number of people they assisted in 2008, with four of the ten provinces (British Columbia, Quebec, Newfoundland and Labrador, and Prince Edward Island) experiencing overall increases (Food Banks Canada 2009a). In 2007 Ontario food banks acquired and distributed 7 million pounds of food across the province to help feed individuals and families (Ontario Association of Food Banks 2008).

Food Banks Canada reports that food banks began 26 years ago as a short-term solution to hunger in Canada. Today, they are a necessary supplement to many caught in Canada's tattered "safety net" (Food Banks Canada 2009b). *HungerCount 2008*, a report of food bank use and users in Canada, revealed

Table I-1   Food Bank Use in Canada by Province, March 2008

Province/Territory	Total Assisted March 2008	% Children	Share of Canadian Total*	Share of Canadian Population**
British Columbia	78,101	31.2%	11.1%	13.3%
Alberta	33,580	42.4%	4.8%	10.6%
Saskatchewan	17,751	45.6%	2.5%	3.0%
Manitoba	40,464	45.7%	5.7%	3.6%
Ontario	314,258	37.6%	44.6%	38.8%
Quebec	156,215	35.7%	22.2%	23.3%
New Brunswick	15,638	33.2%	2.2%	2.3%
Nova Scotia	16,915	35.0%	2.4%	2.8%
Prince Edward Island	2,892	35.4%	0.4%	0.4%
Newfoundland and Labrador	27,260	38.4%	3.9%	1.5%
The Territories	1,340	37.9%	0.1%	0.1%
Total	704,414	37.1%	100.0%	100.0%

Source: Food Banks Canada 2009a, 6.

*The province's share of the national total when it comes to food bank use.

**The province's total population as a share of the total Canadian population. The difference between column 4 and column 5 reveals a higher concentration of need in Manitoba, Ontario, and Newfoundland & Labrador. In other words, there is a proportionately higher use of food banks in these three provinces, in relation to the number of people who live there.

that 50.8 percent of food bank users in 2008 received social assistance cheques that clearly do not cover basic needs; 12.7 percent received disability support cheques, again, that were not enough for sufficient and adequate food;[2] and perhaps most surprising, a growing percentage of food bank clients reported employment as their primary source of income (Food Banks Canada 2009a). *HungerCount 2008* reported that the percentage of working poor who use food banks has more than doubled since 1989, from 6 percent in 1989 to

14.5 percent in 2008 (Food Banks Canada 2009a). These recent national statistics reveal that people with jobs make up the second largest group (after people on social assistance) of food bank users in the country—up 1 percent since 2007.[3] This tells us that there are many Canadian adults who are in the labour force but not earning enough to live and eat. And their children are severely disadvantaged as a result.

Among the increasing number of food bank users, children remain over-represented. In 2008, 37.1 percent of users of food banks were children under 18 (Food Banks Canada 2009a).[4] Some of these children lived in single-parent families—still one of the most economically vulnerable groups in the country. Some 27.3 percent of food bank users across Canada are living in single-parent households, most of which are headed by women.

All of this suggests that welfare and other social assistance programs in Canada, which continue to fall below Statistics Canada's Low-Income Cut-Offs, do not do enough to ensure food security for many Canadians. It also shows that Canada has a shortage of stable, full-time jobs that pay liveable wages.

Homeless families?

The lack of affordable housing is another major issue compounding the child poverty "problem" in Canada. A study highlighted by the Canada Mortgage and Housing Corporation (CMHC) indicates that homelessness is spreading throughout Canada, and that families with children are increasingly among the homeless (CMHC 2003a). After reviewing the existing literature and interviewing 74 agency informants across the country, as well as 59 families who were or had been homeless, the study reported an increase in the number of homeless families requesting services (including emergency accommodations) over the past 5 years in 9 out of the 10 cities surveyed.

Homeless families were defined as families with one or more children under the age of 18 living and sleeping on the street; sleeping in emergency shelters, hostels, or transition houses; living in transitional or second-stage housing; temporarily staying with others; or renting a hotel/motel room by the month (CMHC 2003a). A study of 112 homeless shelters across the country revealed that children were living in many of these shelters. Over half of these children were under the age of 5, almost 30 percent were between the ages of 5 and 12, and less than 15 percent were teenagers (CMHC 2001).

The 2003 report cited several causes of rising family homelessness in Canada, including lack of affordable housing, lack of access to social housing, increasing poverty, changing job markets that contribute to little or no income, family violence, lack of support services, political indifference, and discrimination (CMHC 2003a). These and related issues will be discussed in some detail throughout this book.

What is poverty?: Children's perspectives

Not all children who live in poverty are homeless; nor do all of them use food banks. The majority of Canadian children living in poverty reside in our communities—silent and invisible. Those who are seen are stigmatized and socially marginalized or excluded. This inevitably has negative consequences for individual children, as we will see in Chapter 3, but also for Canada as a whole. Our exceptionally high child poverty rates send out the messages that we do not care; that our perception of ourselves as Canadians is not in line with reality; and that Canadian "values" do *not* include social justice, fairness, inclusion, co-operation, and equality.

Canadian children are voicing their perspectives on poverty. For those not yet convinced that Canada has a child poverty "problem," they may want to read the responses of children in grades four and five to the question: what is poverty? They told us that poverty is:

> ❯ "Wishing I could go to McDonalds"
> ❯ "Getting a basket from the 'Santa Fund'"
> ❯ "Not getting to go to birthday parties"
> ❯ "Wishing you had a nice house"
> ❯ "Not being able to have your friends sleep over because we can't buy snacks or give breakfast"

> ❯ "Not having breakfast sometimes"
> ❯ "Sometimes it's hard because my mom gets scared and she cries"
> ❯ "Not being able to afford a holiday"
> ❯ "Not having pretty barrettes for your hair"
> ❯ "Not having your own backyard"
> ❯ "Being teased for the way you are dressed"

Source: Interfaith Social Assistance Reform Coalition 1998

In this book we will look at just how many of Canada's children live in poverty, exploring trends over time, across provinces, and among various groups. We will see which Canadian children are most vulnerable to poverty and why, and read about the impact of poverty on child development and its outcomes. We will also look at some of the ways that poverty is measured in this country and around the world, and consider Canada in an international context to assess how the country compares—and why. We will uncover the importance of the year 1989 to child poverty in Canada and conclude with a look at the attempts (and failures) to tackle child poverty and the suggestions for improvement—in the hope of, indeed, making Canada one of the best places in the world to live.

Defining and Measuring Child Poverty

What is Child Poverty?

For decades, Canadian politicians and policy makers have been talking about prosperity and productivity. Recently, discussions have introduced a new *pp*: *poverty* (Torjman 2008). While Canada has made progress on reducing poverty rates among seniors, it has been significantly less successful in decreasing poverty among younger Canadians, and particularly among families with young children (see Table 1-1).

Defining *poverty* is very complex, but defining *child* is equally challenging. Canadian legal and policy documents have defined the term *child* as anyone under the age of 6, 7, 12, 14, 16, 18, and 19, depending on the document, policy, program, or jurisdiction. For the most part, however, many national and international agreements define *child* as anyone under the age of 18. Relating age to poverty, statistics reveal that the age of the child, as well as the number of children of specific ages, affect family poverty rates (see Table 1-2). For example, having a number of younger children, and particularly having children under the age of seven, significantly increases the odds of living in poverty, especially in female-headed, single-parent families (National Council of

Welfare 2007c; see Table 1-2). But recently, we rarely talk about *family poverty*.

Table 1-1   Poverty by Age, 2004

| | Number of Persons Living in Poverty | | Poverty Rate | |
	Before-Tax LICO*	After-Tax LICO	Before-Tax LICO	After-Tax LICO
All persons	4,838,000	3,479,000	15.5%	11.2%
Under 18	1,196,000	865,000	17.7%	12.8%
18–64	3,097,000	2,396,000	15.1%	11.7%
65 and older	545,000	219,000	14.0%	5.6%

Adapted from: National Council of Welfare 2007b

* LICO refers to the Low-Income Cut-Off, a way of measuring whether a family has to spend too large of a proportion of its income on basic necessities such as food, clothing, and shelter, compared to other Canadian families (discussed in detail, below).

Table 1-2   Poverty Rate by Number and Age Group of Children, 2004

| | Two-Parent Families <65 | | Single-Parent Mothers <65 | |
Number and Age Group of Children	Before-Tax LICO	After-Tax LICO	Before-Tax LICO	After-Tax LICO
One child				
Less than 7 yrs old	7.9%	4.4%	58.1%	46.6%
7–17 yrs old	8.4%	4.8%	34.0%	22.6%
Two children				
Both less than 7 yrs old	7.2%	4.4%	80.4%	63.0%
One less than 7; one 7–17	9.2%	5.9%	60.4%	49.6%
Both 7–17 yrs old	8.7%	6.6%	36.1%	28.9%
Three or more children				
All less than 7 yrs old	15.0%	10.7%	87.9%	84.9%
At least one less than 7 and one 7–17	23.8%	16.8%	74.5%	60.5%
All 7–17 yrs old	10.9%	9.2%	65.7%	45.5%

Source: National Council of Welfare 2007c

Why *child* and not *family* poverty?

Poverty is widespread in Canada, but only recently is it receiving public attention if it is connected to the terms *children* or *child*. Almost all child poverty is family poverty, but promises to stop poverty attract more attention, and almost all-party government approval, when it is connected to children. Combating child poverty involves a "stronger buy-in than general anti-poverty measures" (Prentice 2007, 58), despite the fact that most efforts to combat it call for supports and services for parents or adults. Some have also argued that the dominant focus on child poverty, particularly in policy discourse, implies that adult poverty is not a cause of social concern (Wiegers 2002).

Wiegers (2002) identifies and discusses a shift in focus from the "feminization of poverty" to "child poverty" in state policy discourse over the last two decades. She argues that the relatively recent focus on child poverty is a result of the restructuring of discourse, connected to policy reorientation. Wiegers explains that the framing of poverty as child poverty is consistent with Canada's new policy orientation that emphasizes enhanced economic growth, international competitiveness, increased reliance on paid work, and individual responsibility. She adds that the emphasis on a child-centred approach to poverty is aimed at alleviating concerns about the impact of this reorientation on the nuclear family, which lacks adequate social supports for parenting, while is still expected to uphold the traditional nuclear family, with a full-time, stay-at-home mother ideal (Wiegers 2002; for a related discussion as it applies to single mothers, see Little, forthcoming).

Consequently, this shift in discourse has had de-gendering and individualizing effects on family poverty (Jenson 2001a); at the same time this coincides with a shift from a paradigm in which parents have full responsibility for their children's well-being—the family responsibility paradigm—to one that has been labelled as the investing in children paradigm (Jenson 2004b; Saint-Martin 2002; Beauvais and Jenson 2001). Reflected in the priorities outlined in Canada's *National*

Children's Agenda (Government of Canada 1997) and *A Canada Fit for Children* (Government of Canada 2002), there is a call for strategies that are child-centred, multi-sectoral, forward-looking, collaborative, and aimed at promoting the basic principles of the United Nations Convention on the Rights of the Child (Government of Canada 1997, 2002). This paradigm shift was due in part to changing state commitment in public and economic policy, but also due to the rise in children's rights activists and experts from civil society (Jenson 2004b).

The increased international attention to children's rights has contributed to a shift in public discourse towards an acceptance of child poverty as a worthy social issue. In contrast to this seemingly progressive shift, the acceptance of *child* over *family* poverty also reflects public thinking, which for the most part continues to separate and blame "undeserving welfare moms"—often associated with family poverty and considered by some undeserving of support and assistance—from deserving, innocent children. As a result, in order to keep poverty on the political agenda, several anti-poverty groups deliberately adopted a child-focused advocacy strategy for more effective media campaigns (Jenson 2004b; Wiegers 2002).

Measuring Child Poverty

Due to the awareness of the large number of children living in straitened or difficult circumstances globally, a number of countries—including Canada—have set specific targets and goals towards the reduction of child poverty, particularly in light of international commitments. But how exactly is poverty measured and how are children living in straitened circumstances counted? There are measures that establish minimum thresholds of resources that help distinguish Canada's poor from non-poor. The "poverty lines" these measures establish represent levels of resources below which it would be insufficient for individuals and families to "normally" participate in society. While these measures do not offer a full portrait of poverty in Canada, they help establish the number of individuals—and in this case, children—who find themselves below the thresholds. In sum, identifying and measuring child poverty in this country involves at least three things: (1) identifying and measuring resources necessary for survival; (2) establishing thresholds that distinguish poor from non-poor; and (3) counting individual adults and children that find themselves below the thresholds (Corak 2006). The following three measures seek to do that. The first two, the low-income cut-off (LICO) and the low-income measure (LIM), are "proportion of typical incomes" measures, involving the calculation of proportion of income levels deemed appropriate or typical for survival—both measures of income (or poverty) calculated in relation to other national incomes. The third, market basket measure (MBM), is a budget study of consumption and costs of resources and is deemed to be a more "absolute" measure of poverty, but it too remains in reference to the wider community and social context.

Since the 1970s, Statistics Canada has been publishing low-income rates based on a low-income cut-off (see Tables 1-1 and 1-2). In Canada this has become one of the most common approaches to measuring low income (Phipps and Curtis 2000)—but no commonly agreed-on measure of poverty currently exists across developed nations (OECD 2005) or within Canada itself (Webber 1998). In fact, Statistics Canada has maintained that the LICO neither can nor should be used as a poverty line (Mendelson 2005). Nonetheless, many have interpreted this measure as such, particularly since Statistics Canada itself has noted that the LICO helps to identify those who are substantially worse off than the average person (Webber 1998).

Low-income cut-offs

Low-income cut-offs have been used for a number of decades as a way of measuring whether a family has to spend too large of a proportion of its income on basic necessities such as food, clothing, and shelter, compared to other Canadian families (making this a relative measure). It was developed using 1959 Family Expenditure Survey data—a survey of household spending. The original calculations found that an average household spent about 50 percent of its pre-tax income on basic food, clothing, and shelter (Albanese 2009b). It was then decided that if a family spent 70 percent of its pre-tax income on these essentials—a somewhat arbitrary 20 percent more than the average families—the family was considered to be in straitened circumstances (National Council of Welfare 2007d; Webber 1998). This threshold—what the average household spent, plus 20 percent—was converted to *a set* of low-income cut-offs that vary by family and community size (see Table 1-3).

Table 1-3   Statistics Canada's Before-Tax Low-Income Cut-Offs (1992 Base), 2007

Family Size	Community Size				
	Cities of 500,000	100,000– 499,999	30,000– 99,999	Less than 30,000	Rural Areas
1	$21,666	$18,659	$18,544	$16,968	$14,914
2	$26,972	$23,228	$23,084	$21,123	$18,567
3	$33,159	$28,556	$28,379	$25,968	$22,826
4	$40,259	$34,671	$34,457	$31,529	$27,714
5	$45,662	$39,322	$39,081	$35,760	$31,432
6	$51,498	$44,350	$44,077	$40,331	$35,452
7+	$57,336	$49,377	$49,073	$44,903	$39,470

Source: National Council of Welfare 2008a

Since this measure was introduced, average household spending on food, clothing, and shelter has declined from 50 percent of before-tax income to about 35 percent before tax, or 44 percent after-tax, resulting in major changes in LICO calculations since 1969 and regular annual updates based on the Consumer Price Index (Webber 1998). Today, LICOs are calculated using either or both pre-tax and after-tax income. A family is typically considered to be living in straitened circumstances if it spends approximately 55 percent (the average of 35 percent plus 20 percent) in the before-tax calculation of LICO, or 44 percent plus 20 percent in the after-tax calculation

(Statistics Canada 2007a) or more, on basic food, clothing, and shelter. Again, this is standardized and calculated based on family and on community size. For example, in 2007 a family of four living in an urban area of 500,000 or more inhabitants was considered to be straitened if it had a before-tax household income of $40,259 (see Table 1-3).

The Low-Income Measure (LIM)

In the late 1980s, the Low-Income Measure (LIM) was introduced for certain types of analyses (National Council of Welfare 2007d; Webber 1998). The LIM is defined as the income equal to half of the family income found in the middle of all families' incomes, or 50 percent of the median income, which is calculated based on family size, not differentiated by community size, like the LICO. It can be calculated on pre- and after-tax incomes, like the LICO. To calculate the LIM, first find the median income. The median income in Canada in any given year represents the middle score or value if all incomes in the country ranked from highest to lowest. Then, find the household income that divides that line in half. The LIM would consider a family to be in straitened circumstances if it has a household income of less than half of the median (middle) income, adjusted for family size. For example, the median after-tax household income for Canadian families with two or more people was $56,000 in 2005 (Statistics Canada 2007a; 2007b). Using the LIM, a family would be considered poor if it had a household income of $28,000 or less (i.e., half of $56,000), regardless of where that family lived (community size).

The LIM is used extensively in international comparisons done by organizations like the Organization for Economic Co-operation and Development (OECD), which documents and compares policies and practices among the most developed and economically advanced nations of the world (OECD 2005).[1] Both LICOs and the LIM are considered to be *relative measures*—measures that compare incomes and deduce that some incomes are considerably lower in relation to others.

Market Basket Measures (MBM)

In 2003 Human Resources Development Canada released another measure of poverty, a budget study or measure, called the Market Basket Measure (MBM). The MBM calculates the amount of income needed by families in order to meet their basic needs. It does this by first estimating the cost of a specific basket of goods and services used by average households in communities across Canada. The MBM is calculated using specified quantities and qualities of goods and services—food, clothing and footwear, shelter, and transportation, as well as other personal and household needs such as furniture, telephone service and modest levels of reading, recreation, and entertainment (National Council of Welfare 2007d). The MBM determines if a person or family's disposable income falls below the cost of the select goods and services in the market basket in their community or in a community of comparable size (see Table 1-4). The MBM accounts for the different needs of families of different sizes and compositions and from different communities and regions of Canada.

Table 1-4   Market Basket Measure (MBM) Thresholds for Two Adults and Two Children, 2000

	Food	Clothing and Footwear	Shelter	Transportation	Other	Total
Vancouver	$6,697	$2,292	$11,020	$1,592	$6,190	$27,791
Calgary	$6,183	$2,156	$8,707	$1,392	$5,743	$24,181
Saskatoon	$6,356	$2,246	$7,096	$1,272	$5,924	$22,894
Winnipeg	$5,972	$2,269	$7,233	$1,601	$5,675	$22,750
Toronto	$5,778	$2,292	$11,399	$2,316	$5,558	$27,343
Montreal	$6,017	$2,269	$7,129	$1,320	$5,706	$22,441
Saint John	$6,499	$2,269	$6,087	$1,340	$6,038	$22,233
Halifax	$6,476	$2,292	$8,241	$1,560	$6,038	$24,607
Charlottetown	$6,335	$2,110	$7,561	$3,612	$5,816	$25,434
St. John's	$6,796	$2,292	$7,298	$1,451	$6,258	$24,095

Source: National Council of Welfare 2004

Some have argued that poverty is much more than low income (Sen 1999); and income-based measures of poverty have many well-known limitations, including the assumption of an equal sharing of financial resources across household members (Kerr and Beaujot 2003). But for the purpose of national and international comparison as income levels are collected and updated regularly, with reasonable reliability, and because they have proven to be a good representation of poverty, many measures are income-based, and most remain "relative" in nature. In noting this, some say that Canada does not have real or *absolute poverty* or a lack of the basic necessities of life, but rather only *relative poverty*—implying that some Canadian children and families only "feel" poor compared to others. However, the experiences and voices of children themselves remind us that poverty in Canada is real. For example, as stated in the introduction, children in grades four and five living in North Bay, Ontario, remind us that whether "real" or "relative," poverty for them means: "feeling ashamed when my dad can't get a job"; "pretending that you forgot your lunch"; "being afraid to tell your Mom you need gym shoes"; "not buying books at the book fair"; "hearing mom and dad fight over money"; "hiding your feet so the teacher won't get cross when you don't have boots"; and "not getting to go on school trips" (Canadian Teachers' Federation 2008, 2). To help contextualize some of these children's feelings, let us consider another measure or concept known as *depth of poverty*.

Overlooked by Some, Unforgettable to Others: The Varying Costs of Home Heating

Some people believe that Canada only has relative poverty—that people only "feel" poor compared to others—but actually have enough to live comfortably. Those with this point of view perhaps have not thought about the high cost of heating and food in some parts of Canada.

The Thunder Bay Economic Justice Committee has compiled information that compares month temperatures in Thunder Bay and in Toronto. Living on low income in Thunder Bay and in northern or more remote communities across Canada could lead one to rethink what is meant by relative poverty.

Heating Degree Days

Thunder Bay has a relatively cold climate and longer heating season, so annual heating costs are higher than in southern Ontario. Therefore the impact of high energy prices is greater in Thunder Bay—especially for those with lower employment incomes as well as homeowners and the working poor. Heating degree days refer to the number of degrees below 18°C the temperature was recorded during a given month. To calculate the number of heating degree days, first find the average temperature by adding the high and the low temperatures for the month and then divide by two. If the number is above 18, then there are no heating degrees that month. If the number is below 18, then subtract it from 18 to find the number of heating degree days.

Table 1-5   Thunder Bay Degree Days Compared to Toronto, 2005

Month	Degree Days Difference Thunder Bay	Toronto	Difference
January	1017.5	752.9	+264.6
February	849.9	662.1	+187.8
March	727.4	571.6	+155.8
April	454.6	353.3	+101.3
May	266.4	171.8	+94.6
June	127.3	49.4	+77.9
July	44.5	8.9	+35.6
August	67.9	17.8	+50.1
September	212.4	102.5	+109.9
October	404.1	282.6	+121.5
November	630.0	445.5	+184.5
December	916.7	647.4	+269.3
TOTAL	5718.7	4065.8	+1,652.9

Source: Brotchie 2006

> Low-income families spend 13.7 percent of their household income on energy, compared to 4 percent of Canadians. At the same time, between 2003 and April 2008, the average price of household heating fuel has increased by 89 percent. Many families living on low-income have faced the difficult choice between heating their homes and feeding their families.
>
> Source: Ontario Association of Food Banks 2008

Depth of poverty, or the low-income gap, is the amount of income a low-income household would need to reach the low-income threshold, or how much it falls short of the relevant low-income cut-off (Statistics Canada 2007a). For example, a family with an income of $15,000, when a low-income cut-off is $20,000, would have a low-income gap of $5,000. It is a measure of how poor Canada's poor really are (Albanese 2009b). Throughout the 1990s, despite a growing economy and changes and increases to the Canada Child Tax Benefit, Canadian families who were poor struggled to survive on incomes that averaged more than $9,000 *below* the low-income cut-offs (Campaign 2000 2002). In other words, on average, low-income families were so poor that they needed about $9,000 to reach the unofficial poverty lines. This gap varies considerably depending on the type of family under consideration (see Table 1-6).

By many accounts, including recent Statistics Canada calculations, the poor are getting poorer and the gap between the lowest- and highest-income families has widened (Statistics Canada 2007a; 2007b). That is, average incomes for the poorest in Canada have increased by about 18 percent ($2,576) over the past 10 years, while between 1994 and 2005, Canada's wealthiest families experienced a 31 percent ($50,115) increase in income (Campaign 2000 2007; Statistics Canada 2007a). Similarly, using Statistics Canada data on wealth, rather than income, Morissette et al. (2002) found that among families whose major breadwinner was aged 25 to 34, median wealth fell by 36 percent. In

Table 1-6   Average Depth of Poverty in Dollars by Family Type, 2004

Family Type	Dollars Below the Poverty Line	
	Before-Tax LICO	After-Tax LICO
Two-parent families under 65 with children under 18	$10,400	$8,500
Female lone-parent under 65 with children under 18	$9,400	$6,300
Male lone-parent under 65 with children under 18	$8,500*	$7,400*
Unattached women under 65	$9,100	$6,700
Unattached men under 65	$8,800	$6,500
Couples under 65 without children under 18	$8,200	$6,300
Couples 65 and older	$3,800	$5,200*
Unattached women 65 and older	$3,200	$2,100
Unattached men 65 and older	$3,400	$3,400*

Source: National Council of Welfare 2007e
Note: Use estimates in italics* with caution. The Coefficient of Variation (CV) is greater than or equal to 16%.

particular, young couples with children experienced significant downward or negative changes as their family's average wealth fell about 30 percent (Morrissette, Zhang, and Drolet 2002). In other words, inequality has worsened among families with children (Ross and Roberts 1999). Since 2000, while the income and wealth gap remained the same, we have started to see some of the lowest poverty rates in close to 20 years (see Table 1-7). However, the recent and rapid downturn in the global economy has and will continue to erode the improvements registered earlier in the decade.

Table 1-7   Poverty Trends, All Persons, 1980-2004

	Number of Persons Living in Poverty		Poverty Rate	
	Before-Tax LICO	After-Tax LICO	Before-Tax LICO	After-Tax LICO
1980	3,850,000	2,807,000	16.0%	11.6%
1981	3,872,000	2,823,000	15.9%	11.6%
1982	4,251,000	3,046,000	17.2%	12.4%
1983	4,631,000	3,478,000	18.6%	14.0%
1984	4,704,000	3,451,000	18.7%	13.7%
1985	4,447,000	3,290,000	17.5%	13.0%
1986	4,202,000	3,098,000	16.4%	12.1%
1987	4,145,000	3,074,000	16.0%	11.9%
1988	3,953,000	2,846,000	15.1%	10.8%
1989	3,719,000	2,704,000	14.0%	10.2%
1990	4,369,000	3,191,000	16.2%	11.8%
1991	4,781,000	3,601,000	17.5%	13.2%
1992	5,062,000	3,677,000	18.3%	13.3%
1993	5,416,000	4,004,000	19.3%	14.3%
1994	5,271,000	3,898,000	18.6%	13.7%
1995	5,530,000	4,185,000	19.3%	14.6%
1996	5,970,000	4,556,000	20.6%	15.7%
1997	5,867,000	4,474,000	20.1%	15.3%
1998	5,466,000	4,024,000	18.6%	13.7%
1999	5,151,000	3,851,000	17.3%	13.0%
2000	4,917,000	3,741,000	16.4%	12.5%
2001	4,711,000	3,394,000	15.5%	11.2%
2002	4,963,000	3,536,000	16.2%	11.6%
2003	4,952,000	3,587,000	16.0%	11.6%
2004	4,838,000	3,479,000	15.5%	11.2%

Source: National Council of Welfare 2007f

Conclusion

Over the past decade we have seen a shift in discourse, from *family poverty* to *child poverty*. At the same time, there is little consensus on what type of poverty Canada has, or how it should be measured. In this chapter we have seen a number of definitions and measures, used differently, in different contexts and with different purposes. Despite their variations, the result is the same; Canada has high rates of poverty. In the next chapter we will explore Canada's child poverty rates, who is most vulnerable and why.

Chapter 2

Child Poverty Rates and Trends

As we will see in more detail in upcoming chapters, Canada's child poverty rates are consistently higher than most other wealthy nations. Since the 1980s, low-income rates in general, and child poverty rates in particular, have roller-coastered their way into the twenty-first century. Child poverty rates dropped from mid-1980 to 1989, increased from 1989 to 1996, began dropping again from 1997 to 2001, and levelled through to 2006 (see Figure 2-1). By 2006, Canada's child poverty rate, excluding poverty in First Nations and select other communities, dropped to 11.3 percent—about the same rate Canada had in 1989 (Campaign 2000[1] 2008). Despite strong economic growth and economic recoveries that followed recent recessions, national child poverty rates over the past two decades have not dipped below the 2006 rates, into the single digits. Child poverty rates are expected to get worse before they get better, with the global economic crisis that started in 2008.

In 2006, 3.4 million Canadians (10.5 percent of the population) lived on low income. Of this, about 760,000 were children under 18 years of age, down from a peak of 1.3 million, or 18.5 percent of all children, in 1996 (Statistics Canada 2008c). Using after-tax income as a measure, one in

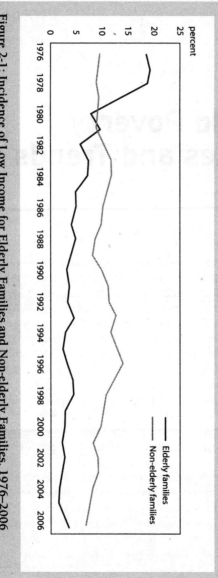

Figure 2-1: Incidence of Low Income for Elderly Families and Non-elderly Families, 1976–2006

Source: Statistics Canada 2008c

nine children in Canada lived in poverty in 2006 (see Figure 2-2). Just over 40 percent of these children lived in households where at least one adult or parent worked full-time for a full year. Over 60 percent (63.5 percent) of children who were poor lived in families in which parents pieced together part-time and/or seasonal work—a variety of work arrangements— to accumulate the equivalent of full-time hours (Campaign 2000 2008). Some children from families that make up the working poor and others whose parents have no income from employment find themselves homeless.

Homeless Children and Families

By a number of estimates, about one in seven users of shelters across Canada is a child, with most using them to escape situations of abuse. In 2001 the Canada Mortgage and Housing Corporation (CMHC),[2] Canada's national housing agency, released a study about children and youth in homeless families. The CMHC conducted a survey of 112 shelters, primarily located in large urban areas across the country. The 112 shelters included 33 general emergency shelters, 64 family violence shelters, and 15 municipal programs that provide temporary shelters, often in motels, to homeless families. While not statistically representative, the study revealed some interesting facts about homeless children in Canada. The CMHC found that over half of the children in shelters in 1999 to 2000 were under the age of 5, about 30 percent were 5 to 12 years of age, and less than 15 percent were teenagers. About 10 percent of families who used shelters had earned incomes, while the rest depended on income support programs, child support payments, or had no income at all. A large proportion of children in shelters shared bedrooms with children and youth from other families, had inadequate study areas, and few counselling services available to them. Thirty-three percent of general emergency shelters, 80 percent of family violence centres, and 22 percent of municipal centres provided counselling for children. In order to leave the shelter system, most families were in need of financial assistance, affordable housing, counselling, life skills training, child care,

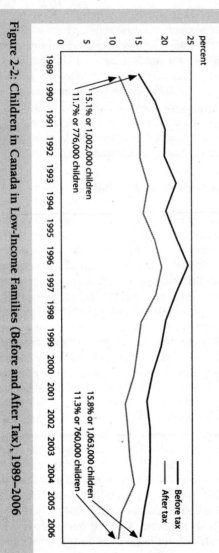

percent

15.1% or 1,002,000 children
11.7% or 776,000 children

15.8% or 1,063,000 children
11.3% or 760,000 children

Before tax
After tax

Figure 2-2: Children in Canada in Low-Income Families (Before and After Tax), 1989–2006
Source: Statistics Canada 2006a

and employment skills. While centres did needs assessments for adults, only half of family violence centres and one-fifth of general emergency and municipal centres conducted needs assessments for the children and youth they admitted (CMHC 2001).

Provincial Variations in Low-Income Rates

The national child poverty rate of 11.3 percent masks considerable provincial variation. Income statistics for 2006 reveal that five provinces had child poverty rates in the single digits: Prince Edward Island (4.0 percent[3]), Alberta (6.9 percent), Nova Scotia (8.7 percent), Newfoundland and Labrador (9.3 percent), and Quebec (9.7 percent). Five others—New Brunswick (11.3 percent), Ontario (11.8 percent), Manitoba (12.4 percent), Saskatchewan (14.4 percent), and British Columbia (16.1 percent)—had rates in the double digits, above 10 percent. Comparing the child poverty rates of the provinces that year, we see that five registered a drop in their child poverty rates (Newfoundland and Labrador, Nova Scotia, Ontario, Manitoba, and Alberta), while five others experienced increases (PEI, New Brunswick, Quebec, Saskatchewan, and British Columbia; see Table 2-1).

Surprisingly, in 2006 the highest child poverty rates were found among some of the "have" provinces, including British Columbia (16.1 percent), which registered the very highest and growing child poverty rate. This was followed by Saskatchewan (14.4 percent), Manitoba (12.4 percent), and Ontario (11.8 percent). Newfoundland and Labrador (9.3 percent), traditionally labelled a "have-not" province, had rates below those considered wealthy or "have" provinces (Newfoundland and Labrador embarked on a poverty reduction strategy; touched upon in Chapter 8). Some of the increases experienced and expected in provinces previously considered "have" provinces, like Ontario and British Columbia, are connected to numerous job losses in the once-prosperous manufacturing and forestry sectors of the Canadian economy. This and other factors will be explored in more detail in Chapter 5.

Table 2-1   After-Tax Child Poverty Rates, 2005-2006

	After-Tax Child Poverty Rate 2005	After-Tax Child Poverty Rate 2006	Difference 2005-2006
Canada	11.7%	11.3%	−0.4%
Newfoundland and Labrador	10.8%	9.3%	−1.5%
Prince Edward Island	3.3%	4.0%	+0.7%
Nova Scotia	10.4%	8.7%	−1.7%
New Brunswick	10.3%	11.3%	+1.0%
Quebec	9.6%	9.7%	+0.1%
Ontario	12.6%	11.8%	−0.8%
Manitoba	14.1%	12.4%	-1.7%
Saskatchewan	12.9%	14.4%	+1.5%
Alberta	8.6%	6.9%	−1.7%
British Columbia	15.2%	16.1%	+0.9%

Source: Adapted and calculated based on Statistics Canada 2006a

Who is Most Vulnerable?

The odds of living in poverty are not the same for all children. In fact, some groups in Canada are considerably more likely than others to live in poverty. In 2005 the most vulnerable group with the highest rate of child poverty was recent immigrant families, where about 1 in 2 (or 49 percent) children lived in poverty. Similarly, about 40 percent of First Nations children living outside First Nations communities lived in poverty. Racialized children (34 percent) and children with disabilities (28 percent) were also more vulnerable compared to other Canadian children. Finally, despite some improvements over time, children living in female-headed, single-parent families remain among the most economically vulnerable, with about 47 percent living in poverty (Campaign 2000 2007).

BC's Child Poverty Shame

On 4 June 2009 headlines across Canada read: "BC still worst in Canada for child-poverty rates." That day Statistics Canada released national child poverty rates and BC ranked last for the sixth year in a row. Provincial coordinator of First Call: BC Child and Youth Advocacy Coalition, Adrienne Montany, was widely quoted stating that despite a drop in 2007, numbers for 2008 are expected to be considerably higher. First Call: BC Child and Youth Advocacy Coalition is a cross-sectoral, non-partisan coalition made up of over 80 provincial organizations and 25 mobilized communities. They include a network of hundreds of community groups and individuals.

First Call: BC Child and Youth Advocacy Coalition, Increased Economic Inequality, Facts, 2009

> Over one in five British Columbian children lives in poverty. That's 21.9 percent or 181,000 children. That is about the same as the combined populations of Nanaimo, Prince George, and Cranbrook.

> The BC rate of child poverty is the highest in Canada, with the national average coming in at 15.8 percent. BC has had the worst record for child poverty five years in a row.

> Child poverty rates between 2005 and 2006 dropped at a national level, but increased in BC.

> Figures show that aboriginal and recently immigrated children have a poverty rate of 49 percent.

> The rate of poverty for BC children in two-parent families has grown to 16.3 percent from a low of 5.4 percent in 1980.

> Government policies make a difference. Without government help, BC ranks sixth for child poverty among the provinces at 29 percent, whereas Newfoundland and Labrador take the last spot at 38 percent. However after government transfers, Newfoundland and Labrador's rate drops to 16.2 percent and BC's only to 21.9 percent, which moves Newfoundland and Labrador into sixth place and bumps BC into last.

> ❭ Government spending is positively correlated with child poverty and does not have a negative effect on global competitiveness. For example, Denmark, Sweden, Finland, and Switzerland all spend more, have a lower child poverty rate, and are more competitive than Canada.

> ❭ Between 1989 and 2006, the richest 10 percent of the Canadian population saw their incomes grow by 30 percent (or $47,591 total). The bottom 10%, however, saw their incomes drop by almost 8 percent (or $1309 total).

> ❭ A report released by the federal Standing Committee on Health says that having low income was the "largest barrier to participation in both unorganized and organized sports" and that this was "particularly true for First Nations and Inuit children"; of the more than 500 First Nations schools, only half have a gym.

> Source: First Call: BC Child & Youth Advocacy Coalition 2009

Mother-led, single-parent families

Despite the recent increase in the proportion of middle-class women choosing to have children (Hertz 2006)—or finding themselves raising children—outside of long-term relationships, most women continue to disproportionately do so in poverty (Kerr and Beaujot 2002; 2003). Family structure or type is one of the most common characteristics among children living in low income in Canada.[4] Showing some improvements by 2006, one in three mother-led, single-parent families lived in poverty (Campaign 2000 2008). Statistics Canada (2008c) reported that almost 310,000 children living in low income lived in single-mother families, representing about 40 percent of all children on low income. This number is down from its peak in 1996, when 56 percent of children living with single mothers were living in a low-income situation (Statistics Canada 2008c).

These mothers face the challenge of having to be the sole provider in a society that continues to undervalue women's paid and unpaid work (for a detailed discussion see Little forthcoming; Little and Morrison 1999). Women are more likely than men to be granted custody of children after divorce and carry a disproportionate share of the care work and volunteer work in our homes, schools, and communities.

With provincial variations, women with young children have been entering the labour force in large numbers, but women still earn approximately 71 percent of what men earn and are more likely to find low-waged and part-time employment (Roy 2006). Women find themselves juggling child care, employment, education and training, and other family responsibilities; and, because they are also less likely than men to remarry after divorce, women are more likely to have to juggle these demands and acquire adequate housing, while raising children on their own. The result is higher rates of poverty among mother-led households.

Using National Longitudinal Survey of Children and Youth (NLSCY) data, Kerr and Beaujot (2002) found that children living in female-headed, single-parent households appeared to be at a relative disadvantage across a number of scales measuring child outcomes; however, they found clear evidence that this was especially related to their low-income status.

Children in Aboriginal families

Another group of children disproportionately likely to live in poverty in Canada are Aboriginal children living both on and off reserves—some of whom are also more likely to live in mother-led households. According to the 2006 Census, some 1,172,790 people identified themselves as Aboriginal, which represents 3.8 percent of the total population in Canada—up from 3.3 percent in 2001 and 2.8 percent in 1996 (Statistics Canada 2009a). In 2006 Aboriginal children were twice as likely to live in a lone-parent family compared to non-Aboriginal children (31 percent of children compared to 14 percent of non-Aboriginal children), and this was especially likely if the family lived off-reserve (Statistics Canada 2008a).

While there were significant improvements to the economic position of Aboriginal Canadians living in some of Canada's larger cities, there was also substantial growth in the proportion of Aboriginal adults employed, but earning less than $15,000 (Statistics Canada 2005a). In 2006 the employment rate for Aboriginal Canadians of working age (25 to 54 years) was 65.8 percent, up from 61.2 percent in 2001 (Statistics Canada 2009a).[5]

As a result of a long history of colonization, assimilationist government policies, and discrimination, Aboriginal Canadians were more likely than other Canadians to have not completed high school (33 percent compared to 13 percent), to have lower employment rates, and to have average incomes far below the national average (Armstrong 2000; Assembly of First Nations 2007a). First Nations families are larger than average Canadian families and households are almost 6 times more likely to be overcrowded (17 percent of households were overcrowded compared to 3 percent of non-Aboriginal households) (Statistics Canada 2008a). As a result of some of these conditions and circumstances, Aboriginal children are also over-represented in the child welfare system (Blackstock et al. 2006; Trocmé, Knoke, and Blackstock 2004).

Aboriginal families have significantly higher rates of poverty, less stable housing, are more likely to be led by younger parents, and are more likely to have parents who were maltreated as children (Trocmé, Knoke, and Blackstock 2004). With the current Aboriginal birth rate at about 1.5 times above the average Canadian rate (Statistics Canada 2005b), and if there is to be little improvement in living conditions on- and off-reserve, child poverty rates among Aboriginal peoples in Canada are predicted to remain high.

Recent immigrants families

Since the early 1990s, about 225,000 people have immigrated to Canada per year. Recent immigrants to Canada gravitate to Canada's largest cities, especially Toronto, and parachute into an uncertain labour market (see Chapter 5). Recent research shows that four years after arriving here, the majority of new immigrants reported encountering many difficulties in finding work (Statistics Canada 2009a). Studies from 2005 reveal that the most frequently mentioned difficulty was lack of Canadian work experience (49.8 percent). This was followed by lack of contacts in the job market (37.1 percent), lack of recognition of foreign experience (36.6 percent), lack of recognition of foreign qualifications (35.4 percent), and language barriers (31.9 percent) (Statistics Canada 2009a; Shields, Rahi, and Scholtz 2006). Along with the high cost of housing and the high cost of living in Canada's largest cities, it is comprehensible that many newcomer families with children find themselves disproportionately likely to live in poverty.

A number of studies have reported that foreign-born, recent immigrant children were twice as likely to live in poverty as children born in Canada (Beiser et al. 2002; Campaign 2000 2007; Palameta 2004; Picot, Hou, and Coulombe 2007). Due to changing immigration policies—with growing emphasis on high levels of education and training, skills, and credentials from the home country—and changing economic conditions in Canada, many very recent immigrants have had a more difficult time finding adequate employment compared to other Canadians and immigrants who arrived before 1995 (CMHC 2009; Citizenship and Immigration Canada 2005). By the end of the last wave of the Longitudinal Survey of Immigrants to Canada (LSIC)[6] in 2005, about 68 percent of study participants—new immigrants—were in the labour force and had an average family income of about $53,000, compared to $62,300 for all Canadian families (CMHC 2009). Low-income rates among recent immigrants in their first year in Canada peaked at 3.5 times that of Canadian-born adults in 2002—a rate higher than at any time throughout the 1990s (Picot, Hou, and Coulombe 2007).

Many immigrants—35 to 40 percent—who arrived in the 1990s were able to exit low income within about a year. Those who entered Canada after 2000 were more likely to experience low income and less likely to exit it soon after arrival (Picot, Hou, and Coulombe 2007). This led to situations of chronic low income—low income in four of the first five years in Canada—for a disproportionate number of newcomer children and families. It also resulted in as many as 22 percent of recent immigrant households being overcrowded, and being even higher for very recent immigrants (CMHC 2009; Citizenship and Immigration Canada 2005). Comparing household size using 2006 Census data and the results from the LSIC, the Canada Mortgage and Housing Corporation (CMHC 2009) found that the average Canadian household had 2.5 people, while newcomers lived in households averaging 3.6 and 3.7 people in their first 4 years after settlement in Canada. Newcomers' households were more likely to include extended family, non-family members or boarders, and/or two or more families living in the same dwelling (CMHC 2009). Early results of the LSIC stated that nearly three-quarters of new immigrants surveyed spent more than 30 percent of their monthly income on housing and half spent more than 50 percent on housing (CMHC 2009). The LSIC also identified significant housing differences across and among visible minority groups, with South and Southeast Asian immigrants having a higher degree of homeownership, while West Asian, Arab, and Black respondents in the survey reported having major difficulties locating housing (CMHC 2009). It should also be said that most newcomers to Canada in recent years are members of visible minorities or racialized groups, which has also contributed to higher than normal rates of low income.

Using data from 1991 and 1996, researchers Abdolmohammad Kazemipur and Shiva Halli (2001) found that belonging to a visible minority group in Canada increases the odds of living in poverty. They point to lower returns on family social class background, education, and work experience of recent immigrants, many of whom are racialized, implying that racial discrimination has contributed to high poverty rates (Kazemipur and Halli 2001).

Big problems in big cities

Most newcomers to Canada settle in one of three major gateway cities: Toronto,[7] Montreal,[8] and Vancouver; and increasingly, second-tier recent immigrant destinations: Edmonton, Calgary,

Winnipeg, Hamilton, and Ottawa (Citizenship and Immigration 2005). Cities are also home to more hospitals, social service agencies, and employment opportunities that are both growing and shrinking. Larger cities are also places of increasing concentrations of people living on low income. For example, the Greater Toronto Area (GTA) has recently been labelled the child poverty capital of Ontario. It received this grim title since half of all Ontario's children living in poverty currently live in the GTA (up from 44 percent in 1997). This is not a recent development. There has been a 30-year upward trend in the after-tax child poverty rates in the Toronto area, with rates doubling in the past 22 years. A recent Children's Aid Society of Toronto study reported that close to half of female-headed, single-parent families (46 percent) and recent immigrant families (44 percent) cannot afford their current housing. Similarly, a United Way study, *Poverty by Postal Code* (2004), that followed a previous study *A Decade of Decline* (2002), charts a rapid and dramatic rise in the number of high-poverty neighbourhoods throughout the GTA. Much of this has to do with the changing economic climate in Ontario (Children's Aid Society of Toronto 2008).

Of the sixteen areas that experienced economic deterioration from 2000 to 2006, nine were in Ontario. Of the five Census Metropolitan Areas (CMA) that registered the largest drops in ranking between 2000 and 2006, four were in Ontario's Golden Horseshoe (Oshawa, Hamilton, Toronto, and Windsor); the fifth was Regina (Akyeampong 2007). Shrinking economic opportunities for Canadian-born and foreign-born urban dwellers are compounded by residing among concentrations of poor neighbours (Smith and Ley 2008). Spatial segregation, high-density public housing, limited employment opportunities, social detachment, and mounting social stigma are increasingly a reality for Canada's urban families that are poor.

Losing Ground, a report on poverty in Canada's largest and nominally wealthiest city—Toronto—noted that between 2002 and 2006, Canada lost nearly 250,000 jobs in the manufacturing sector,[9] which meant the loss of high-wage permanent jobs with low education requirements. The report adds that by 2002, an estimated 37 percent of the Canadian workforce was employed in temporary, low-waged, unstable, "non-standard" jobs, which minimize labour costs to employers. Temporary work wages are on average 16 percent lower than permanent work wages (MacDonnell 2007). For more details, see Chapter 5.

Hidden poverty in rural and semi-rural communities

While child poverty rates in cities like Toronto are over double the national rate, it is not uncommon for this to be true of child poverty rates in many small cities, towns, and rural communities across Canada. For example, Renfrew County, a large rural county in Eastern Ontario, had one in eight children living in poverty in a recent count. One of its largest cities, Pembroke, Ontario, had no less than 26.2 percent of children under the age of 18 living in poverty. During the last recession, almost one in every two children under the age of six was living in poverty in Pembroke (CPAN 2009). Not surprising, child poverty rates vary greatly across small communities, with pockets of deep poverty in some areas, surrounded by cottage or recreational, retirement, and suburban communities.

Much of this is due to the fact that in many rural and semi-rural areas, education and employment opportunities are limited (one-resource or industry towns, for example), often requiring travelling long distances by car. Many of the available jobs are unstable: seasonal, part-time, and often low paid. In Renfrew County, for example, just over half of all employed have full-time jobs that last the full year; the rest hold part-time and/or seasonal jobs. In 2005 the median after-tax income for couples with children was $10,000 below the provincial median ($64,803 in Renfrew County compared to $74,095 for Ontario; Statistics Canada 2009e). To make matters worse, the seasonal and unstable nature of some rural jobs make many ineligible to qualify for Employment Insurance benefits.

Despite having access to specific numbers, rates, and trends, much less is known about the characteristics of poverty in rural and semi-rural communities. For example, while large cities struggle with the "concentration" of poverty, some rural communities struggle with the "isolation" of poverty—among many other issues. Urban dwellers rarely contemplate the impact, intersection, and consequences of being poor and having disproportionately high heating costs with few heating options, restricted access to health care, social services, and housing, all compounded by little or no public transportation.

Conclusion

There is no question that children are poor because their parents are poor. But contrary to popular belief, many of these children live in families where at least one parent is employed, although many of these parents earn only minimum wage or close to that. It is widely known that no matter where in Canada a family lives, one person earning minimum wage, working full-time, full-year is not enough to allow that family to live above the poverty line. It also is widely known that living in poverty puts children at a disadvantage in a number of areas and ways. The next chapter will explore the impact of poverty on children. The chapters that follow will explore the causes of high poverty rates in more detail.

Chapter 3

Incomes and Outcomes

The Impact of Poverty on Children

By almost every measure, poverty has been found to have far-reaching negative consequences. There is ample evidence that as family incomes fall, risks of poor developmental outcomes in children's health, learning, and socialization increase (Howe and Covell 2003; Robson-Haddow 2004; Ross and Roberts 1999). Statistical and other analyses reveal that higher income—regardless how income is measured—is almost always associated with better outcomes for children. The relationship between monetary incomes and child outcomes is most significant among younger children. Income increases considerably impact Canada's youngest children within families at very low income levels (Phipps and Lethbridge 2006). What does low income mean in the lives of young children?

Young children depend on others for their well-being. Healthy development includes access to basic nutrition and safe neighbourhoods (Jones et al. 2002; Kerr 2004). Lower income contributes to limited access to adequate housing; and inadequate housing often means overcrowding, strained living conditions, residential instability, and poorer and less safe neighbourhoods (McCartney et al. 2007). Parents who are poor are less able to purchase products and services to help their children with their learning, and often cannot afford recreational activities that promote physical, social, emotional, and intellectual development. The alternative results in sedentary activities, such as watching television, often with negative effects on children's health and their well-being (Berry 2007; Burdette and Whitaker 2005; Kerr 2004). The physical and developmental risks for children associated with economic disadvantage have been well documented, with higher physical health scores, for example, having consistently positive associations with family incomes (Phipps and Lethbridge 2006).

Physical Outcomes

While the majority of children born in developed nations enjoy unprecedented levels of health, the wealthiest nations in the world are not necessarily the healthiest (UNICEF 2007). The obstacles are in the amount of poverty amid prosperity, or income inequality, and the lack of social programs aimed at combating poverty. Some have found the link between family income inequality and poor physical health to be so consistent that they have argued that it is effectively a natural law: greater income equality within a society, or, less of a gap between the wealthy and the poor, results in better health outcomes for the entire society (Chung and Muntaner 2006; Wilkinson 2005). Despite some variations, studies show that child poverty negatively impacts physical outcomes, including mortality, morbidity, accidents, and abuse (Bradshaw 2002). In fact, some of the impact of poverty on health is evident from birth, if not in utero (Howe and Covell 2003).

Poverty has been found to increase the odds of pregnancy complications for mothers living in poverty (Whitehead et al. 2009). Research from the United States has found that white women living in communities with high unemployment, low education, poor housing, low proportion of managerial or professional occupations, and high poverty were associated with increased odds of pre-term birth, with similar but smaller effects for black women (Messer et al. 2008).

Urquia et al. (2007) point out that socio-economic disparity in birth outcomes are one of the most persistent findings in perinatal research. They note that there is abundant evidence of an association between several measures of low socio-economic status and adverse birth outcomes across a number of countries, including Canada—which has universal health care.

Studies of health outcomes in early childhood have found that compared to other infants, those in households with lower incomes were more likely to be judged by their mothers not to be in excellent health and were more likely to have been admitted to hospital. One study concluded that low household incomes are associated with poorer overall health and higher hospital admission rates among infants within the first five months of life, even after adjustment for factors known to affect infant health, including a mother's level of education (Séguin et al. 2003). A follow-up to this study found that hospitalization risks for children living in the most severe poverty group resembled that of the non-poor group, while children living in less severely poor families were more likely to be hospitalized. These results suggest that even in Canada, with universal health care, there are health differences among different groups of children, and there are hospitalization barriers for children living in chronic and severe poverty (Nikièma et al. 2008).

With or without universal health care, it is widely accepted that poverty is one of the most influential factors affecting illness. Ross, Roberts, and Scott (2000), for example, found that children in low-income families were over 2.5 times more likely to have problems with vision, hearing, speech, or mobility than children in high-income families. Studies have also shown that poverty and its connection to limited opportunities for physical activity within a safe environment affect the rate of illness in general and the risk of obesity and Type 2 diabetes in particular (Dean and Sellers 2007; Phipps et al. 2006). The quality of food consumed is also linked to these physical illnesses.

Socio-economic disparities in nutrition have been well documented (Howe and Covell 2003; McIntyre, Walsh, and

Connor 2001).[1] For example, a study conducted among Canadian households (1986–2001) found a persistent and, in some circumstances, growing gap between household income and the nutritional quality of food purchases (Ricciuto and Tarasuk 2007). In addition, food expenditures—at stores and in restaurants—were lower among low-income households compared with other Canadian households. Low-income households purchased fewer servings of milk products, fruits and vegetables, and meat and meat alternatives compared to high-income Canadian households (Kirkpatrick and Tarasuk 2003). Also, while children made up about 25 percent of Canada's poor in 1998, they made up over

The Cost of Healthy Eating

The short and long-term trends in food prices are significantly magnified in remote reserve communities in Ontario. Retail prices are absolutely staggering for many foods in Northern communities accessible only by train or air. The cost of groceries including milk, potatoes, and beef can be up to 180 percent greater than retail prices in the average Canadian grocery store. It is not an unusual sight to see 20 diapers for $25, a bag of oranges or flour for $10, or a case of baby formula for over $50. It is likely that the cost of all foods in these isolated communities will continue to escalate with the price of airline fuel, as much must be transported in via plane.

Our fellow Ontarians living in communities from Fort Severn and Sandy Lake to Landsdowne House and Moosonee have to pay a great price to put good food on their tables. This is particularly troubling given the communities' economic circumstances, which place severe limits on affordability, as well as the increased prevalence of chronic health conditions such as diabetes, which makes healthy food choices a matter of survival.[2]

Median household income for Aboriginal women in Canada is $15,883 per year; median household income for Aboriginal men is $21,268 per year. A significant proportion of on-reserve Aboriginal Ontarians receive social assistance (22.5 percent of on-reserve Aboriginals versus 5.5 percent for the general population in Ontario; National Council of Welfare 2007a).

Table 3-1   Price of Selected Food Items, Canadian Average Versus Remote Northern Reserve Communitie in Ontario, April 2008

Food Item	Price Per Unit		
	National Average	Remote Reserve Average	Difference
orange juice (1 L)	$3.67	$3.82	+0.15
wieners (450 g)	$2.71	$4.55	+1.84
apple juice (1.36 L)	$1.83	$2.77	+0.94
corn flakes (675 g)	$3.94	$8.17	+4.23
peanut butter (500 g)	$2.55	$3.82	+1.27
oranges (1 kg)	$2.17	$5.27	+3.10
potatoes (4.54 kg)	$3.97	$11.29	+7.32
bananas (1 kg)	$1.43	$4.11	+2.68
flour (2.5 kg)	$4.69	$9.38	+4.69
eggs (1 dz)	$2.56	$3.34	+0.78
apples (1 kg)	$2.95	$6.79	+3.84
baby food (128 ml)	$0.59	$1.26	+0.67
bread (675 g)	$2.43	$3.70	+1.27
chicken (1 kg)	$5.76	$9.91	+4.15
ground beef (1 kg)	$6.10	$8.29	+2.19
milk (1 L)	$1.96	$2.90	+ 0.94
TOTAL	$49.31	$89.37	+40.06

Source: Ontario Association of Food Banks 2008

42 percent of people using food banks (Howe and Covell 2003). All of this inevitably results in different health outcomes for children in low-income households. The health effects of this are compounded by limited access to physical activity.

In a cross-sectional study, mothers in 20 American cities were asked to report on the average time of outdoor play and television viewing of their 3-year-old children. They were also asked about their perception of their neighbourhood's safety, and their children's body mass index (BMI) were also measured. Of the over 3000 children studied, 35 percent lived in households with incomes below the US poverty threshold. The study found that children who lived in neighbourhoods that were perceived by mothers as the least safe watched more television. But in this case, television watching and minutes of outdoor play were not found to be significantly correlated to BMI and risk of obesity (Burdette and Whitaker 2005).

On the other hand, a number of studies have noted that television viewing varies along class lines, with less well-off families averaging more television watching than white-collar families (Berry 2007; Roberts and Foehr 2004); the same was found for obesity rates (Phipps et al. 2006). Other studies revealed that children between the ages of three and six who watched a large amount of TV were susceptible to early-onset obesity as television viewing substituted physical activity, which in turn reduced energy expenditure relative to energy in-take, leading to obesity (Dennison, Erb, and Jenkins 2002; Rose and Bodor 2006). Children who watched more television were also more susceptible to persuasive advertisements for food of poor nutritional value (Lewis and Hill 1998), leading to unhealthy food preferences, dietary imbalance, and obesity (Utter, Scragg, and Schaaf 2006). In sum, television watching remains a relatively economical source of entertainment for families of low incomes, compared to other types of organized activities for children, and it also contributes to inactivity and unhealthy eating.

Children from more affluent families have more access and exposure to activities at home, including reading and participation in organized sports, as well as other lessons, which predict and positively affect greater readiness to learn (Verdon 2007; Thomas 2006). Children themselves have recognized this. For example, an American study (Fortier 2006, 123) of children's views on poverty cites one child who said:

> If she has friends in the neighborhood, maybe she'll be able to play with her friends in the neighborhood, instead of like kids who do probably have a lot more money get to go out places, like roller

skating, maybe Six Flags, maybe go to other countries for a vacation. She'll probably just be able to stay in her neighborhood and play with her friends since her parents don't have much money for her to go other places and have more fun.

Reflecting on how children living in poverty can spend their summer vacation, another child in the study added:

> He probably gonna just watch TV and stuff and then go to bed . . . They can eat . . . then they go to sleep, then they wake back [up] and do the same thing. He want to . . . play for the basketball team because it's boring at his house and he ain't got nothing to do except do the same thing over and over and then he didn't have enough money and then he didn't join the basketball team (Fortier 2006, 123).

Children from lower-income households are also more prone to injury, most likely due to housing and neighbourhood conditions (Olsen et al. 2008). The *Canadian Medical Association Journal*, for example, has noted that while there was a decline in the rate of unintentional injuries among Canadian children living in urban areas between 1971 and 1998, children who were poor were still twice as likely as children in affluent homes to die of an unintended injury (Stanwick 2006). This finding, along with the other health-related factors, leaves children living in and with low income at a disadvantage compared to other children. Negative physical outcomes further contribute to increased challenges with behavioural, emotional, and cognitive development.

Cognitive Outcomes and School Readiness

A child's health affects his or her cognitive development and school participation, such that poor health can lead to poor participation, irregular attendance, and high rates of school drop out (Howe and Covell 2003; Sridhar 2009). Low income has been found to have a particularly strong association with cognitive (Peabody Picture Vocabulary Test scores and others) and behavioural outcomes very early in life (Phipps and Lethbridge 2006).

Ross and Roberts (1999), in analyzing data from the 1994–95 wave of Canada's National Longitudinal Survey of Children and Youth (NLSCY), found that over a third of all children living in low-income households exhibited delayed vocabulary development compared to less than 10 percent of children in high-income families. Early childhood poverty subsequently affected continued schooling such that children who were poor were less likely to graduate from high school compared to children who did not experience poverty or experienced it later in childhood (Brooks-Gunn and Duncan 1997). Williamson and Salkie found that both before and after near Canada-wide welfare reforms that introduced mandatory welfare-to-work initiatives, preschool children in working-poor families had higher school readiness scores than their peers whose families received social assistance. But preschool children in both working and non-working poor families had lower scores on the Peabody Picture Vocabulary Test–Revised (PPVT–R, a measure of school readiness) than children in non-poor families (Williamson and Salkie 2005). Similarly, another analysis of NLSCY data found that household income was a significant predictor for many measures of five-year-old children's readiness to learn at school (Verdon 2007; Thomas 2006).

Once in elementary school, these patterns persist. For example, a Statistics Canada analysis of grade three Ontario Education Quality and Accountability Office (EQAO) standardized test results by Tremblay, Ross, and Berthelot (2001) found that students from higher socio-economic backgrounds performed better than those from lower socio-economic status backgrounds. Scores were also higher in schools located in higher socio-economic status (wealthier) neighbourhoods. Through these and numerous other studies, it has become clear that all Canadian children are not stepping into the elementary school system on equal footing, and as a result, some have lower success rates and rates of school completion (Brooks-Gunn and Duncan 1997). This inevitably affects opportunities and choices into adulthood and is a cause for concern and attention.

Jennifer Robson-Haddow reminds us that perhaps one of the most threatening outcomes of poverty is the risk of children who are poor growing up to be adults who are poor. She notes that poverty in Canada has intergenerational links that cannot be broken by income assistance alone and, in fact, may be worsened by current income assistance programs or welfare. She adds that low-income families are actually discouraged from saving—if that is even possible—because asset tests restrict their eligibility for provincial welfare programs. This means that applicants must deplete most of their savings before they can qualify for benefits and they risk losing benefits if they begin to save (Robson-Haddow 2004). This puts parents of children living in poverty in very uncertain and distressing situations, further straining their ability to cope and to parent effectively.

Parental Distress and Parenting in Poverty

Poverty results in social exclusion; and social exclusion magnifies problems associated with poverty. For example, because of limited resources parents living in or with low income often have a difficult time providing their children with nutritional food and adequate clothing and housing, resulting in increased stress (Beiser et al. 2000). More significantly, these parents are often blamed for the conditions in which they find themselves. For example, parents considered "high risk" by child protection services[3] are often working hard to raise children in poverty but are nonetheless identified as requiring improved parenting skills. At the same time, parents' perceptions of their own needs are typically not sought. Russell, Harris, and Gockel conducted a longitudinal study of 35 parents over an 18-month period, focusing on low-income parents' views on barriers to effective parenting. Their study revealed that parents consistently identified poverty as the primary barrier to their ability to provide adequate care for their children. At the same time, parents accepted personal responsibility for their economic and parental failings (Russell, Harris, and Gockel 2008).

Parents acknowledged that depression and despair associated with the poverty they experienced impaired their parenting and increased self-doubt about their parenting skills (Russell, Harris, and Gockel 2008). Other studies have confirmed this as well.

Maternal responsiveness to children has been found to vary by socio-economic status (Brooks-Gunn and Markham 2005).[4] Low family income has been associated with maternal emotional distress, strained parenting practices, and family stress, all of which affected parents' ability to cognitively stimulate children (McLoyd 1998; Yeung, Linver, and Brooks-Gunn 2002). There are some women with children who find themselves living in poverty as a result of relationship breakdown and divorce. These women are expected to parent effectively at a time when their emotional and economic circumstances have significantly changed—at a time when they are least able to provide emotional support for others, including for their children (Nair and Murray 2005; Rotermann 2007).

For others, limited health literacy, or the extent to which one can access and interpret health information, acts as a barrier to effective parenting while living in poverty. This is prevalent among those of lower socio-economic status. Porr, Drummond, and Richter (2006) suggest that health practitioners and those working with low-income families should consider better equipping low-income mothers with the necessary knowledge and skills to gain control over their lives and optimize the healthy development of their children. This could help alleviate some stress among mothers and improve health outcomes of children. At the same time, some of mothers' distress is the result of the stigma that our society places on people, and especially parents, living in poverty. For example, one analysis suggests that lone mothers have been established, discussed, and described as "other," "welfare bums," and "flawed consumers" without the financial resources to participate in consumer society (Breitkreuz 2005; Little 1998; Little and Morrison 1999; Power 2005). These types of attitudes support myths and heighten parental distress when parents already find themselves in strained circumstances. Many of these studies underscore the importance of providing low-income parents with understanding, support, employment and/or educational opportunities, and access to programs that will assist them in alleviating their own distress in difficult times.

Parents and Cultural Capital

Living in poverty affects a child's access to financial means, obviously, but often affects social and cultural capital, as well (Kerr and Beaujot 2002). Cultural capital refers to having access to the know-how of socially approved and valued practices connected to high social status and prestige (Bourdieu and Passeron 1977). Middle-class parents are often more likely than parents living in low income to have access to this socially valued know-how, which includes the verbal and linguistic competencies, public performance, and culturally approved social skills that are so often associated with "success" as adults and parents (Lareau 2000). Middle-class parents are more likely to have the resources necessary to deliberately encourage their children's talents in order to optimize their aptitudes in school, sports, etc., and ultimately in their careers (Kusserow 2004). Middle-class parents pass on this know-how and ability to navigate middle-class values and norms to their children, which in turn get rewarded in schools by teachers. Because low-income parents have less access to this know-how, their children are often at a disadvantage on this front, in school and later in life.

Weininger and Lareau (2003) also found that while not all middle-class parents were equally assertive, they tended to talk more, took control of their child's education more effectively, and more overtly challenged the authority of teachers than did parents from more economically disadvantaged backgrounds. As a result, middle-class parents were able to influence the educational system more and advocate on behalf of their children to gain more individualized academic attention for them. Middle-class parents not only had the economic resources for tutors, computers, study space, trips, etc., that gave their children advantages, but also had the social status, authority, and knowledge of the dominant discourse, or cultural capital, as well.

Children of Immigrants and Immigrant Children Faring Better than Others

As noted in Chapter 2, recent immigrant or newcomer children are significantly more likely than non-immigrant children to live in families whose income falls below regional poverty lines. But, studies also show that they are less likely than other children in Canada to experience emotional and behavioural problems (Beiser, Hou, Hyman and Tousignant 2002; Beiser, Shik, and Curyk 1999). It has been found that some of the social pathologies associated with poverty among children are less common in immigrant families. On the other hand, immigrant children with depressed mothers or in unstable families tend to handle racial harassment at school less well, are less likely to succeed at school, and are more likely to become delinquent (Beiser, Shik, and Curyk 1999).

Why do immigrant children tend to fare better in poverty compared to other children? Research shows that it is not simply *current* income that needs to be understood as connected to child outcomes, but rather *permanent* (sustained and long-term) income that is especially important (Blau 1999). The duration and developmental timing of poverty have been found to be important factors when it comes to child outcomes. Children in persistently poor families had the lowest levels of performance on tests of language and school readiness. As well, chronically poor families were more seriously and consistently disadvantaged compared to those in temporary poverty (National Institute of Child Health and Human Development Early Child Care Research Network 2005). Given that current immigration policies require most parents or adults to enter Canada with higher than average educational credentials, and generally higher socio-economic status, poverty is a new situation for many immigrants, experienced only after their arrival and unemployment or underemployment in Canada.

Beiser et al. (2000) found that simply moving out of poverty did not appear to be sufficient to improve children's developmental outcomes unless it was accompanied by substantial improvement in living standards. On the other hand, while income *changes* (ups and downs) appeared to be less important for child outcomes than income *levels*, especially among older children, income changes were found to be particularly important for children's emotional scores (Phipps and Lethbridge 2006).

Importance of Communities

There is also growing evidence that child behavioural and emotional problems are not only influenced by each individual and family, but also by characteristics of the neighbourhoods in which children live. O'Brien et al., for example, found anxiety and depression levels differed significantly across neighbourhoods even after accounting for family socio-economic status differences. They found that children who lived in neighbourhoods with high degrees of physical and social disorder, a fear of crime, and a fear of retaliation had higher levels of anxiety and depression than children living in other neighbourhoods. Higher potential for community involvement for children in their neighbourhood was associated with fewer behavioural problems among children in economically impoverished neighbourhoods. They also found that differences in parenting behaviour did not appear to influence neighbourhood effects on children's behaviour problems (O'Brien et al. 2008).

Conclusion

Children living in low-income families are not "destined" to live deprived lives. Not unlike O'Brien et al. (2008) and Jones et al. (2002) noted, the effects of long-term poverty on children are influenced and decreased by neighbourhood resources and/or social capital. They found that the local norms of some neighbourhoods, and particularly those with more social supports, can positively modify the effects of long-term poverty. Similarly, children who are poor and live in families with constructive and supportive relationships also have an advantage (Kerr 2004). In fact, numerous studies show that children in low-income families benefit from parental supports in the form of high-quality child care (Esping-Andersen 2007; McCartney et al. 2007; Prentice 2007), anti-poverty programs (Gassman-Pines and Yoshikawa 2006), targeted welfare programs (Gennetian and Miller 2002), and a host of other national- and neighbourhood-based initiatives (Bradshaw 2002). This problem is complex, and explanations for why poverty exists and persists are varied and abundant, as we will see in the coming chapters. Consequently, a range of initiatives are needed in order for improvements to take place. Some of the causes of poverty will be discussed in the next three chapters, followed by options and proposals for improvement.

Chapter 4

Exploring Causes I

Family and Neighbourhood Factors

When measuring and discussing child poverty, it is actually the incomes and related conditions of *adults* that are being measured and compared. It stands to reason that children are poor because the adults who care for them are poor. To understand the causes of child poverty, it is important then to try to understand why Canadian adults are poor. By doing so, we will better understand the intergenerational transmission of poverty, and some of the life paths that are set in motion early in life.

While it is not uncommon to hear some Canadians blame individual adults and parents for the economic circumstances in which they find themselves, a large body of research shows that the causes of child and family poverty include demographics or family circumstances, neighbourhood characteristics, labour market forces and relations, and government policies (Chen and Corak 2008). These factors, on their own and in combination, have resulted in Canada's disproportionately high rate of child poverty. We begin by exploring demographic, family-level, and neighbourhood factors below. Labour market forces will be discussed in Chapter 5 and government policies in Chapter 6.

Demographic and Family-Level Factors

For the most part, Canadians are postponing marriage, having fewer children, and are choosing to have them at a later stage in life (Kerr and Beaujot 2003). More mothers are older and more likely to have some post-secondary education and to be working for pay when they have their first child (Healthy Child Manitoba 2003). A Statistics Canada study found that while women with children earned substantially less than women without children (and the gap widened with an increase in number of children), mothers who had their first child at age 30 or later had earnings that were higher than mothers who had children at a younger age, and even higher than some who were childless (Zhang 2009).

Parents, and especially mothers, who have children at a younger age are less likely to pursue post-secondary education, and are more likely to be unemployed or underemployed, in lower-paying, less stable jobs. Some women who become pregnant before the age of 25, while not at greater medical risk, are considered to be at increased social, economic and lifestyle risk (Tough et al. 2006). Under the best of circumstances, Canadians between the ages of 15 and 24 have had, and continue to have, among the highest unemployment rates in the country; they also had the lowest median wages in the country, at $10.00 per hour (Statistics Canada 2009a). As a result, Canadian women who have children at a younger age, particularly if they are single mothers, are more likely than other women to live in or on low income (Kufeldt 2002). Many are poor because they are young, less well-educated, less likely to find higher-paying employment, *and* lone mothers.

Changes in family structure and family law in Canada

Following the liberalization of divorce laws in 1968, and again in 1985, the number of children in Canada who have had to experience their parents' divorce has increased. With rising rates of divorce, more children find themselves temporarily or permanently living in single-parent households. This has resulted in a large number of children living in poverty. In fact, some have argued that about two-thirds of the change in child poverty rates since the 1980s may be due to the increase in the number of lone-parent families resulting from divorce (Kerr and Beaujot 2003).

Over that period, there also has been a rise in the number and proportion of cohabitation or common-law unions in Canada, which are more likely to be shorter in duration than marriages, and more likely to end. As a result, more than 60 percent of children born into common-law families will experience their parents' separation by the time they turn 10, compared to just under 15 percent of those whose parents married without living together first (Department of Justice 2002). This, too, has contributed to the rise in number of single-parent families—some of which are poor.

In 2006 there were 1,132,290 female-headed single-parent families, up from 589,435 in 1981. While many of these are older (61 percent in their late 30s and 40s in 2006, compared to 43 percent in 1981), more likely to have completed high school (82 percent in 2006, compared to 51 percent in 1981), and more likely to have some post-secondary education (44 percent in 2006, compared to 29 percent in 1981), there are still some that are disproportionately likely to have low average earnings, particularly if they are under the age of 25 (Vanier Institute of the Family 2009; see Figure 4-1).

Living in a lone-parent household does not always lead to poverty. As a matter of fact, countries with the lowest child poverty rates, like Sweden, also have high rates of female-headed, lone-parent families. Clearly, it is not lone parenthood but rather lone parenthood in conjunction with other factors—factors such as maternal age and level of education at the individual level, and other broader social factors including limited economic opportunities and rigid or limited family and social policies—that contribute to higher than average poverty rates in Canada.

Preventing adults from leaving unhappy and conflict-ridden relationships will not improve matters; neither will it necessarily improve parenting practices or improve child outcomes. For example, Strohschein (2005), using NLSCY

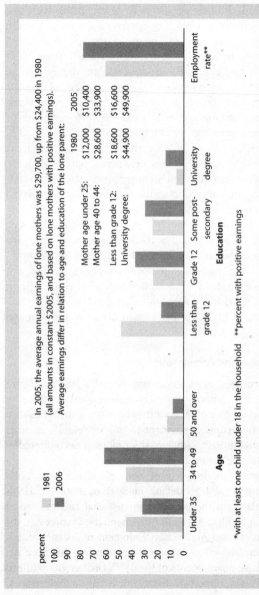

In 2005, the average annual earnings of lone mothers was $29,700, up from $24,400 in 1980 (all amounts in constant $2005, and based on lone mothers with positive earnings). Average earnings differ in relation to age and education of the lone parent:

	1980	2005
Mother age under 25:	$12,000	$10,400
Mother age 40 to 44:	$28,600	$33,900
Less than grade 12:	$18,600	$16,600
University degree:	$44,900	$49,900

*with at least one child under 18 in the household   **percent with positive earnings

Figure 4-1: Lone-Parent Mothers*: Age, Education, and Employment Rates, 1981 and 2006

Source: Vanier Institute of the Family 2009

data, tracked children ages four to seven, living with two
biological parents in 1994. She compared the mental health
of children whose parents remain married from 1994 to
1998 to those whose parents divorced by 1998. Strohschein
found that even before the marriage breakup, children whose
parents later divorced exhibited higher levels of anxiety,
depression, and anti-social behaviour than children whose
parents remained married. She found that socio-economic or
financial resources and the quality of adult relationships in
the pre-divorce period fully accounted for poorer children's
mental health in the initial interview period, among children
whose parents later divorced. In other words, socio-economic
factors and parental conflict in the pre-divorce period played
a key role in child outcomes (Strohschein 2005). Making
divorce harder to obtain would not likely eliminate children's
high levels of anxiety and anti-social behaviour while the
parents are together. Conditions for children do improve,
however, if in the post-divorce period children have regular
and positive contact with both parents and if child support
payments are made regularly, in full, and on time (Juby et al.
2005; Dunn et al. 2004; Bauserman 2002; Wallerstein and
Kelly 1980).

Child support and default rates

Single parenthood in itself does not inevitably lead to poverty,
as experiences among older, more educated mothers in
Canada and in some other countries have revealed. Let us then
consider child support payment rates and defaults as other
factors that compound some of the problems encountered in
the post-divorce period.

Unacceptably high levels of non-compliance with child
support orders, or, high default rates, throughout the 1990s
— particularly on the part of non-custodial fathers—led to
the creation of Bill C-41, an Act to Amend the Divorce Act, the
Family Orders and Agreements Enforcement Assistance Act,
and the Garnishment, Attachment and Pension Diversion Act
(1997). These amendments of the 1985 Divorce Act outlined
the federal child support guidelines, including a simple series of

tables specifying the amount of child support to be paid by the non-custodial parent based on the payer's income (Department of Justice 2006). The legislation was designed to support the efforts of various new provincial enforcement agencies created to help locate spouses in breach of support orders and agreements. The provincial enforcement agencies were allowed to collect funds from income tax refunds, employment insurance benefits, old age security payments, GST credits, etc., under federal jurisdiction. However, less than half of all child support cases are registered with a maintenance-enforcement program to assist with the collection of child support at the provincial level (Robinson 2006).

According to NLSCY data, children covered by private child support agreements, arranged by both parents privately, are more likely to receive regular child support payments compared to children whose parents have a court-ordered agreement. Sixty-six percent of children whose parents had a private agreement received regular payments compared to only 43 percent whose parents had court-ordered agreements. Children who lived in common-law unions that dissolved also were less likely than those whose parents were legally married before the marriage breakdown to receive regular child support payments, whether payment arrangements were private agreements or court-ordered (Department of Justice 2002).

A number of analysts have found a link between the frequency of contact between non-custodial parents (mostly fathers) and their children and the regularity of child support payments (Department of Justice 2002; Juby, Le Bourdais, and Marcil-Gratton 2005; Marcil-Gratton and LeBourdais 1999). In other words, non-custodial fathers who saw their children at least once a week were much more likely to make payments regularly and on time than were those who rarely or never saw their children (48 percent compared to 7 percent; Department of Justice 2002). Others with less frequent or no contact were more likely to default on payments and contribute to higher than average child poverty rates among post-divorce, lone-parent families.

Neighbourhood Effects

While neighbourhoods alone do not cause poverty, they profoundly shape the lives and experiences of their inhabitants (Power 2007) and can contribute to the continuation of intergenerational cycles of poverty. Low-income families are often forced to live in neighbourhoods with underfunded schools, a lack of access to social services, higher than average crime rates, pollution and traffic, and a lack of amenities for children and youth (Kazemipur and Halli 2000). Living in neighbourhoods that are poor does not inevitably condemn its residents to a life of poverty, but living in high-density, poorer neighbourhoods tends to increase children's chances of having anxiety problems, being a part of delinquent subcultures, and having fewer positive peer influences that encourage pro-social behaviour (Amato and Zuo 1992). The two latter points or processes are called the "transmission by percept," where a child's exposure to attitudes, actions, and conditions is so frequent that they become part of, or have a profound impact upon, his or her own outlook (Kazemipur and Halli 2000; Wilson 1996).

Some people living in high spatial-concentrated poverty in urban areas may also develop a subculture or consciousness distinct to the circumstances. This is not meant to blame or criticize inhabitants of these areas, as some have interpreted— or rather misinterpreted—Oscar Lewis' (1964; 1966; 1968) concept of "subculture of poverty," but rather it is meant to acknowledge some of the complex, collective responses to the impact of poverty's everyday uncertainty (Harvey and Reed 1996). Similarly, Caughy, Nettles, and O'Campo (2008) identified and discussed the existence of neighbourhood social processes that compound and allow for the continuation of poverty. They explain that the high negative social climate in some neighbourhoods contribute to children's behaviour problems, which in turn are likely to lead to academic failure, higher dropout rates, and increased chances of involvement in delinquent behaviour. They also found that while positive parenting was important for child outcomes,

Community Co-operation and the Work of CPAN

The Renfrew County Child Poverty Action Network, better known as CPAN, is a network of over 250 individuals from diverse cultural and socio-economic backgrounds, ranging from members of the working poor to a senator and 57 member organizations at the local, provincial, and national level. It was formed in 2000, with a mandate to increase the awareness of the extent and effects of child poverty in communities across Renfrew County—a large, rural county in Eastern Ontario. Its goal is to take action, practically and politically; to improve the lives of children and families; and to promote a vision of a Renfrew County where all children belong.

CPAN is action-oriented and has adopted a multi-pronged approach that includes a range of practical assistance programs, education and training, advocacy, and a firm commitment to social inclusion. Since 2000, members of CPAN have made presentations to community groups and political leaders, developed public education materials, liaised with the media, and provided advocacy and links to resources for many low-income families and their children. They have assisted children with school supplies and shoes through their Backpack Plus Program (under threat due to funding cuts and government fiscal restructuring), with snowsuits and boots through their Operation Snowsuit Program, and with participation in recreational and cultual activities through fundraising.

A Community Affair: Operation Snowsuit

One example of CPAN's initiatives is Operation Snowsuit, which provides a snowsuit, boots, hats, and gloves to children in need of them. In 2006 CPAN distributed 148 snowsuits; in 2007 this increased to 207; and in 2008 it increased again to 273. The program is self-sustaining and is run *by* the community, *for* the community, and *in* the community. That is, the CPAN coordinator personally sends out a letter to the county's directors of education, who, with their blessing and encouragement, forward two letters to local schools. The first goes to school principals, announcing the annual launch of Operation Snowsuit. The second letter comes in two parts, and is sent home with all children in elementary and secondary schools in the district. The first half of the letter asks for donations of clean, gently-used snowsuits, gloves, etc.; the second half provides a contact number urging families in need to contact CPAN and provide details on the sex, size, and number of snowsuits required.

All donated items are picked up by Bell Canada volunteers or employees, who then drop them off at a local Giant Tiger store, whose store owner has donated a part of their warehouse space for the items. Once at Giant Tiger, the items are sorted, repackaged, and labelled by volunteers, who pass them on to Bell Canada employees, who deliver them to pick-up points throughout the county. Last year, the program served newborns to youth aged 18. Unfortunately, with each passing year, the need for Operation Snowsuit has been growing; fortunately, so too is the community's response and generosity.

CPAN's ultimate goal is to be awarded the UNICEF designation of being a "child friendly" county. If members of CPAN have their way, they will succeed.

Source: Renfrew County Child Poverty Action Network (CPAN) 2009

neighbourhood-concentrated economic impoverishment and the negative social climate that often accompanies it, had its own independent, negative effect on children's behaviour. In other words, "child behaviour problems are not only a function of processes at the individual and family level but are also influenced by characteristics of neighbourhoods in which they live" (Caughy, Nettles, and O'Campo 2008, 47).

Neighbourhoods, housing quality, and children's well-being

The Canada Mortgage and Housing Corporation (CMHC) conducted a study (2003b) of the impact of housing quality on children's behaviour problems. The study found that a number of children's behaviour problems were significantly related to the physical condition of the child's room, kitchen, living room, and bathroom, as well as the overall condition of their residence's exterior and general physical condition of the neighbourhood. They found that in all cases, spaces and

Canada Lacks Housing Strategy

Toronto Star, 5 March 2008

Housing is one of the most basic needs. Yet federal Finance Minister Jim Flaherty's only acknowledgement of that in his budget speech last week was to say that Canadians "want healthy, safe communities." His budget did nothing to help low- to middle-income families get and keep housing they can afford.

Monte Solberg, the federal minister responsible for housing, thinks so little about the file that he skipped out on a housing ministers' meeting last month. His reason: he needs to count the number of social housing units in the country before he can talk to the provincial ministers about it. They could have told him there aren't nearly enough and they're deteriorating rapidly.

The lack of action on social housing was highlighted last week in Toronto when a 50-year-old homeless man froze to death in a downtown parking lot stairwell, his crutches beside him.

At their last federal-provincial meeting in 2005, the housing ministers issued principles for an affordable housing framework and agreed to work quickly on a strategy with goals, timetables and long-term funding. But, with the change of government since then in Ottawa, none of that has developed.

Indeed, the only current federal housing programs were brought in by the previous Liberal government and extended by the Conservatives. They are all set to expire a year from now. Housing activists had hoped at the very least that Flaherty would commit to extending those programs, which have provided $1.6 billion for affordable housing, assistance to landlords to upgrade aging social housing stock, and $135 million a year for services and transitional housing for the homeless.

But the only money in the budget was $110 million for five pilot projects across the country to study homeless people who are mentally ill. As Michael Shapcott, director of community engagement for the Wellesley Institute, points out: "Increasing knowledge is critically important, but so too is building affordable homes with the appropriate supports for people with mental health concerns."

Affordable homes are equally important to the 1.5 million Canadian households that are spending more than 30 per cent of their pre-tax income on housing. The costs of homes and rents outpaced inflation every year from 1997 to 2005.

Some 170,000 Ontario households are stuck on waiting lists for social housing, including 3,650 households in Durham, where Flaherty's own riding is situated.

Canada is the only major country in the world without a national housing strategy. Until the federal government commits to devising one with the provinces, living conditions for Canadians will continue to deteriorate and despair and hardship will grow.

Source: *Toronto Star* 2008

neighbourhoods with more physical problems were connected to more behavioural problems in children. In sum, housing and neighbourhood quality had a strong link to childhood behaviours and accounted for 12.7 percent of the difference in behaviour problems of children (CMHC 2003b). As noted above, behaviour problems in childhood can and do lead to lower educational achievement levels and an increased risk of low-income adulthood. In addition to housing quality, access to healthy food choices can also add to problems when there is a high spatial concentration of poverty.

Neighbourhoods and access to healthy food choices

Smoyer-Tomic et al. (2008) examined whether exposure to supermarkets and fast-food outlets varied with neighbourhood-level socio-economic status in Edmonton, Alberta.[1] The study found that the odds of exposure to fast-food outlets were greater in areas with more Aboriginal inhabitants, renters, lone parents, and low-income households. Edmontonians living in low-income neighbourhoods were 2.3 times more likely to have a fast-food outlet within a 5- to 10-minute walk compared to those in more affluent neighbourhoods, and had fewer opportunities to reach food retail outlets outside their neighbourhood. While supermarkets were not found to be systematically absent from low-income neighbourhoods, the study explained that due to industry trends towards larger, more profitable grocery stores, we have seen more store closures in "mature" urban neighbourhoods and the construction of fewer, larger stores in cheaper suburban locations, where land is more readily available. The study found that Edmonton's residents who were poor had higher exposure to low-cost, energy-dense foods that likely contribute to a higher prevalence of obesity and other negative health consequences (Smoyer-Tomic et al. 2008).

Socio-economic differences in diet are well documented, and American research shows there are fewer healthy choices available in stores in poorer neighbourhoods and retail prices tend to be higher (Crockett, Clancy, and Bowering 1992; Horowitz et al. 2004). An Australian study of food accessibility and neighbourhood socio-economic disadvantage found that advantaged neigh-bourhoods were better off in terms of access to fruit and vegetable stores. Those in advantaged neighbourhoods also had the greatest number of food stores within a two-kilometre radius from home, travelled the shortest distance to the nearest supermarket, and had the greatest selection of healthy food items (Ball, Timperio, and Crawford 2009). Despite variations in urban core redevelopment, and the resurgence in popularity of socially mixed public housing projects (August 2008), this issue is so widespread that we have seen the rise in the use of the term "urban food deserts" (Mead 2008). Increased costs and challenges associated with accessing fresh food contributes to negative health consequences that result from poor diet. There are other related negative health consequences, including pre-term births.

American research found that living in highly populated areas with high unemployment, low education, poor housing, low proportion of managerial or professional occupations, and high poverty were associated with increased odds of pre-term births for non-Hispanic, white women (Messer et al. 2008). The prevalence of pre-term births, and the possible subsequent poor health outcomes for children, can further strain household resources and worsen economic problems. Such environments also negatively impact existing life stresses and chronic strains, particularly among parents who may be additionally concerned about their children's safety and well-being (Amato and Zuo 1992).

Conclusion

So far, we have considered some individual-, family-, and neighbourhood-level explanations and factors that cause or intensify child poverty in Canada. When focusing on individuals, families, and communities, it is often easy to forget the wider social, political (public policy), and economic factors that help to create and maintain the low-income status quo. In the next chapter we will turn to some of these broader issues—namely the changing economy and public policies—that add to the discrimination and social exclusion of Canada's low-income families.

Chapter 5

Exploring Causes II

Canada's Changing Economy

Causes of child and family poverty are numerous, complex, and intertwined. Demographic or family circumstances and neighbourhood characteristics are connected and best understood in relation to changing labour market forces and government policies. This chapter will examine some of these larger-scale forces, and particularly Canada's changing economy, and their involvement in the perpetuation of Canada's high child poverty rates.

Labour Market Forces and Relations

According to Statistics Canada (2009a), there have been two periods of sustained declines in employment in Canada over the past three decades: in the 1981–1982 and 1990–1991 recessions. Statistics Canada explained that the decline in employment was "major but shorter-lived" in the recession of the early 1980s; while the drop in employment in 1990–1991 was less severe, it had effects that lingered in the labour market for a longer period of time. It was not until 1994 that employment rates returned to their pre-recession levels. During the recession of the early 1980s, the unemployment rate

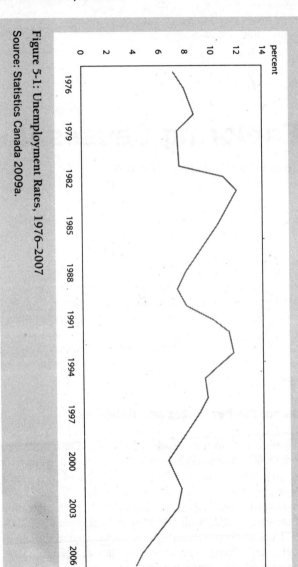

Figure 5-1: Unemployment Rates, 1976–2007
Source: Statistics Canada 2009a.

increased from 7.6 percent in 1981 to 12.0 percent in 1983; during the recession of the early 1990s, the unemployment rate was 11.4 percent in 1993 (Statistics Canada 2009a; see Figure 5-1). When not in the middle of recessions, it is not uncommon for employers to rely on temporary lay offs, therefore forcing workers onto Employment Insurance as a means of adjusting to periods of depressed sales (Corak and Pyper 1995).

Child poverty rates mirror the ups and downs that accompany periods of national economic prosperity and recessions. For example, child poverty rates began to drop immediately following the recession in the early 1980s. Child poverty rates reached a low point in 1989, only to rebound during the following recession in the early 1990s. Because employment "recovered at a snail's pace" after the recession of the early 1990s (Statistics Canada 2009a, 12), child poverty rates began to drop only in the latter half of the 1990s, reaching 1989 levels by 2006–8. Child poverty rates will inevitably reach new highs following the most recent set of global economic crises starting in 2008–9 (see Sauvé 2008 for predictions).

Almost every census metropolitan area (CMA) across Canada experienced increases in the number of people receiving regular Employment Insurance (EI) benefits in 2008–9; the number of people receiving regular EI benefits in Canada rose by 560,400 or 4.4 percent between December 2008 and January 2009 (Statistics Canada 2009b). In one year, between February 2008 and January 2009, the number of EI beneficiaries climbed 22.8 percent, with over half the growth occurring in Ontario (see Figure 5-2). Most of this was due to job losses, especially in Canada's manufacturing sector, and will inevitably translate into higher child poverty rates, especially in Ontario, after late 2008 and early 2009.

It is not solely high unemployment rates that have contributed to high child poverty rates. Some people, who are employed both part-time and full-time, find themselves unable to move out of poverty. How and why has this been possible during seemingly "prosperous" economic times?

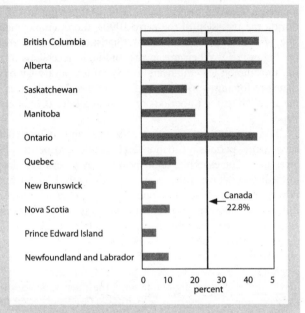

Figure 5-2: Percentage Change in Number
of People Receiving Regular Benefits,
February 2008–January 2009

Source: Statistics Canada 2009b

Recession, 15,000 Job Losses Forecast: Alberta Finance Minister
CBC News, 19 February 2009

Alberta is facing a recession and 15,000 lost jobs, Finance Minister
Iris Evans announced Thursday in her latest economic update.

"After years of robust economic growth, the provincial economy is
forecast to contract by two per cent over this next year," Evans said.

The province is running a deficit estimated to be about $1 billion,
but money left over from the 2007–08 fiscal year will be used to
make sure government departments have enough money.

"That's going to supplement the revenue, take the place of revenues we'd have had from the Heritage Trust Fund ... and help us offset what otherwise would be more of an operating deficit."

Evans was reluctant to discuss the $1-billion figure at Thursday's news conference, saying more definite figures will come when she releases her third-quarter economic update next week.

Alberta legislation prohibits the government from running a deficit.

NDP Leader Brian Mason said Evans is not being clear about what's going on.

"I don't think she's being straight with Albertans about this not being a deficit," Mason said. "This is not a deficit as defined by the act, and that's why I said, she doesn't have to go to jail, but really it's a deficit."

Mason accused the government of contributing to the province's budget woes by levying low resource royalty rates when oil prices were high.

Alberta Liberal finance critic and Calgary MLA Dave Taylor also had questions about Thursday's update.

"I'd like to see a budget. I'd like to see some details. I'd like to see some numbers.... I'd like to know whether this is a real deficit, a technical deficit or a hypothetical dollar deficit," he said.

World economy to blame: province

The province is blaming low energy prices and the global credit crunch for the change in the province's economic fortunes.

The province estimates job losses will raise the province's unemployment rate to 5.8 per cent from last year's rate of 3.6 per cent.

Evans is forecasting the economy will improve at the beginning of 2010.

The news marks a dramatic turn in Alberta's finances. Just last summer, when oil was at a high of $147 US a barrel, the province was forecasting an $8.5 billion surplus.

The drop in crude oil prices—crude for March delivery is now trading at less than $40 US a barrel—and turmoil in the world economy put a dent in that surplus. By the end of the second quarter on Sept. 30, the projected surplus had shrunk to $2 billion.

Source: CBC News 2009

Unemployment's Silent Effects

David is an injured, unemployed worker.

For David, being unable to provide for his family was a source of overwhelming embarrassment. He discussed how at his lowest point he had so seriously contemplated suicide that he had laid clothing on his bed he wanted to be buried in:

> I was in a major depression. Suicidal ideation. I get chills even going back there. On the bed was my suit, a shirt and a tie—because my wife can't pick out ties at all. My plan was done. And that's it. I thought this is the only way I can provide for my family in a monetary sense. Life insurance. I'd rather have died than do what I was doing.

Source: Brotchie 2007

Changing employment trends

It is not surprising to read that employment levels in Canada hit an all-time high in 2007 (Statistics Canada 2009a), almost precisely at the time when child poverty rates reached 1989 lows of 11.3 percent (Campaign 2000 2008). Some of the increases in employment levels and rates have come with the rise of women's labour force participation, which rose by 120.5 percent between 1976 and 2007, compared to 45 percent for men over the same period (Statistics Canada 2009a; Roy 2006). By 2007, almost half (47.3 percent) of all workers were women compared to 37.1 percent in 1976 (Roy 2006; Statistics Canada 2009a; Statistics Canada 2007c). There is no doubt that a driving force in this increase is the result of improvements in the status of women in Canada since the 1970s. At the same time, much of this increase has occurred because of economic necessity and rising income insecurity (Albanese 2009a).

Over the past five years, the largest employment gains were in the service sector—which happened to disproportionately benefit women. In 2007, 88.4 percent of employed women worked in the service sector compared to 65.5 percent of employed men (Statistics Canada 2009a). The service sector includes finance, insurance, real estate, business services, other support services, public administration, educational and health services, and retail sales. As there was a rise in service-sector employment, Canada experienced declines in the male-dominated goods-producing or manufacturing sector (Gera and Mang 1998). In fact, during the recessions of the 1980s and 1990s, men experienced steeper and more prolonged employment declines than women, as manufacturing and construction were especially hard hit (Statistics Canada 2009a). As a result of employment sector shifts, the unemployment rate for women (5.6 percent in 2007) has been consistently lower than that for men (6.4 percent in 2007) since the late 1980s (Statistics Canada 2009a; Statistics Canada 2007c).

While some initially see this as positive news for Canada's children, especially for children in female-headed families, the fact is that the rise of the service sector and the decline of the manufacturing sector and construction trades have also meant a drop in the number of relatively high-paid, often unionized jobs with good benefits packages that require relatively little education compared to some of the "new," often lower paid, and more unstable jobs in the service sector (Albanese 2009a). Even in 2007, as the manufacturing sector continued to experience declines, Statistics Canada reported that wages were significantly higher in manufacturing, with the average hourly wage for factory work of $21.11, compared with that of $15.39 in trades (Statistics Canada 2009a).

When Statistics Canada (2009a) carved the economy into two broad industry classes (the goods-producing, manufacturing industries and the service sector), it found that the average weekly earnings of workers tended to be considerably higher in goods-producing industries, with average weekly earnings of $977 in 2007, compared to the services, with average weekly earnings of $716 that same year (see Figures 5-3 and 5-4).

The two branches of jobs and earnings and rising income inequality

There is no question that we find ourselves in "a digital economy, an information economy, an internet economy, an innovation economy, a high-tech economy, a real-time economy, and a global-economy" (Statistics Canada 2004). In Canada's new economy the "ability to create wealth is increasingly dependent on the effective management of knowledge ... the organizational capability to create, acquire, accumulate, disseminate, and exploit information and knowledge" (Gera and Mang 1998, 150). The share of employment of knowledge workers has increased in all regions of Canada, and knowledge workers have become "a highly-prized commodity" (Statistics Canada 2004). Many of the leading growth industries in Canada between 1986 and 1991 were linked to communication technology and services, followed by business and community/social/ personal services. While there was an increase in the demand for knowledge workers, it also is well documented that there has been a division within the service sector into two branches, and a polarization of jobs and earnings (Hughes and Lowe 2000; Lowe 2000; Myles 1988). That is, while some of the new jobs are high-skilled and knowledge-based, many of the new jobs being created in Canada's new economy are low paid, low status, and part-time—or what some have colloquially and controversially termed "McJobs" (Albanese 2009a).

Growth in retail sales jobs

With the globalization of production and trade, many manufacturing jobs have moved "south" or overseas, to parts of the world where workers are paid considerably less than Canadians. These global economic shifts resulting in the decline of the manufacturing sector have added downward pressure on the earning capacity of Canadians—especially on those without post-secondary education (Statistics

Canada 2008c). At the same time, the rise in the proportion of Canadians working in the service sector has come with increased demand for post-secondary education, but has not always resulted in better paid and more stable employment opportunities. In fact, the largest employment sector in this country in 2007 was retail and wholesale trade, which employed about 2.7 million people that year. About three-quarters of these, or about 2 million Canadians, worked in retail trade. Since the early 1990s the largest retail employers were food and beverage stores, employing one in four retail workers. General merchandise stores had the second-largest number of workers, followed by clothing and accessories stores (Statistics Canada 2009a). By 2007 the most prevalent occupation in Canada for both men and women was retail salesperson.

In 2006 nearly 285,800 men in Canada reported that they were retail salespeople or clerks, an increase of 28.6 percent from 2001 to 2006. This was followed by truck driver (276,200 men), the second-largest occupation, which was up 17.4 percent since 2001 (Statistics Canada 2009a). Women, too, reported retail sales as the most prevalent job, at just over 400,000. This was followed by cashier (255,500). In 2007 sales and service occupations accounted for 29.3 percent of all working women over the age of 15; another 2.2 million women (27 percent) worked in business, finance, and administrative occupations (Statistics Canada 2007c). A considerably smaller number of women worked in jobs connected to social science, education, government service, religion, and health occupations (Statistics Canada 2009a).

Unionization

Many of the new jobs created within the service sector, particularly in retail sales, are non-unionized; others, in the public sector, have seen a rise in unionization. In 2007 4.5 million Canadian employees were covered by a collective agreement, up 17.3 percent from 3.8 million in 1997; however, this growth has not kept pace with the growth in number of employees over the same period. That is, in 2007,

31.5 percent of all workers were covered by a union contract, down from 33.7 percent 10 years earlier. The drop was especially noticeable among male workers aged 25 to 54 and among workers in the private sector. By all accounts, unionization is associated with higher earnings, such that by 2007 the average hourly wage of unionized workers was $23.51, compared with $18.98 for non-unionized workers (Statistics Canada 2009a). As we see growth in retail sales, we can expect a growth in lower-waged, non-unionized jobs.

What this means for Canada's children is that a growing proportion of them have parents not holding higher-paid, relatively stable manufacturing or other unionized jobs, but instead are employed in lower-paid, often part-time or less stable jobs in sales and related services. A growing proportion of their parents also find themselves having to hold multiple part-time jobs to make ends meet. Since 1976 the number of Canadians working at two or more jobs has more than quadrupled from 207,000 to 891,000 in 2007. Multiple-job holders accounted for 5.3 percent of all workers in 2007, up from 2.1 percent in 1976 (Statistics Canada 2009a).

Growth in part-time and temporary employment

While more Canadians work full-time compared to part-time, over the past three decades the number of Canadians working part-time has increased sharply, more than doubling over the same period. As a matter of fact, between 1997 and 2003 temporary work grew much more rapidly than permanent work (Galarneau 2005). By 2007 nearly one in five workers—over 3 million workers—were employed part-time compared to one in eight in 1976 (Statistics Canada 2009a). Furthermore, a growing proportion of Canadians were employed in temporary jobs, making up 12.9 percent of all workers in 2007, compared to 11.3 percent in 1997. The majority of these work in limited-term or contract jobs, often through a temporary help agency.

Those having contract employment made up the bulk of temporary workers in 2007—amounting to 6.6 percent (or 935,000 workers) of all employees. This was followed by casual workers, making up 3 percent (or 475,000), and seasonal employees, also at 3 percent (or 417,000 workers) of all employees (Statistics Canada 2009a). More men worked in seasonal employment, while more women worked in casual, contract employment.

A growing proportion of Canadian workers, and especially women, were classified as self-employed (Statistics Canada 2007c). While this often sounds impressive, implying independence, the average income of those who were self-employed in 2005 was $16,767 ($20,080 for men and $12,000 for women); some 79 percent of all self-employed have incomes of less than $20,000 (Statistics Canada 2009a).

Most Canadians who are self-employed work on contract, are casual workers, or take part in what has been termed non-standard employment. They are generally less well paid, have fewer employee benefits, are offered less on-the-job training, and are in unstable job situations, resulting in earnings instability and income-related stress for their families— including their children. In 2003 temporary workers earned 16 percent less than permanent workers, with average hourly wages of $16.69, compared to $19.98 for permanent workers; seasonal, casual, and those employed through temporary agencies earned 28, 24, and 40 percent less, respectively (Galarneau 2005). This gap, coupled with earnings instability, often results in Canadian families putting off making large purchases and longer-term decisions, particularly in regards to housing. It can also make getting approval for loans and credit more difficult to obtain.

Wages "rising"?

Statistics Canada (2009a) research revealed that in 2007 Canadian employees earned an average of $20.41 per hour before taxes and other deductions—up 3.5 percent compared to 2006 (see Figure 5-3). However, after adjustments for inflation, wages in Canada rose only 1.3 percent that year. Slight increases were registered for the past four years, but before that, real average hourly wage after being adjusted for inflation declined 0.6 percent from 2002 to 2003 (Statistics

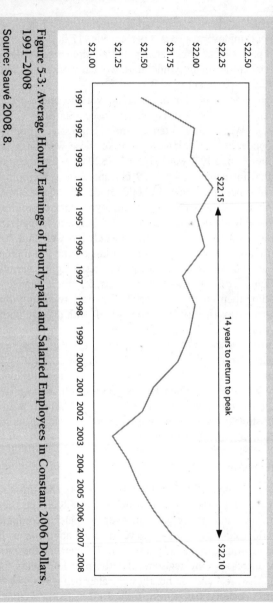

Figure 5-3: Average Hourly Earnings of Hourly-paid and Salaried Employees in Constant 2006 Dollars, 1991–2008

Source: Sauvé 2008, 8.

Canada 2009a; Statistics Canada 2008c). There also have been significant provincial variations.

Over the past decade, Alberta's strong economy has positively affected average hourly wages, which rose 6.1 percent in 2007 alone (3.8 percent, when adjusted for inflation)—making Albertans the highest hourly earners in the country. Workers in Nova Scotia and Newfoundland and Labrador also experienced increases in real hourly wages of about 3 percent, but their average hourly wages of $17.35 and $17.46 respectively remained below the national average. Having said that, Newfoundland and Labradorians had the smallest rise in the cost of living (1.5 percent), resulting in an increase in their purchasing power (Statistics Canada 2009a)—a value undoubtedly reflected in their dropping child poverty rates. British Columbia, the province with the highest child poverty rates in the country in 2005–6, was the only province whose median hourly wage declined from $19.73 in 1997 to $19.00 in 2007 (Campaign 2000 2008; Statistics Canada 2009a). Quebec's median hourly wage remained fairly steady during the same period, hovering between $16.72 and $17.00; their child poverty rates similarly remained constant.

In 2007, while the proportion of employees earning $30.00 or more climbed 4.7 percent across Canada, or 17.8 percent of workers, one out of two employees was earning less than $18.00 an hour. Though they still had a higher median wage than workers with less education, between 1997 and 2007 employees with an education above the bachelor's level experienced a 1.8 percent decline in their median wage in 2007 constant dollars to $29.12. As a point of comparison, employees with master and doctoral degrees earned an average of $30.44 per hour in 2007, 75 percent more than employees with a high school diploma, who earned on average $17.37 per hour (Statistics Canada 2009a).

Workers in sales and services, the largest employer of men and women in Canada, have the lowest wages, averaging $13.65 per hour in 2007 (Statistics Canada 2009a; Statistics Canada 2008c). Some of the lowest paying jobs, all in the service sector, registered average weekly earnings under $500.

These included workers in accommodation and food services ($324); arts, entertainment, and recreation ($454); and retail trade ($486) (Statistics Canada 2009a; see Figure 5-4). They also made up a large proportion of employers in Canada.

Statistics revealed that in 2005, Canadian employees who earned wages and salaries earned on average $36,703 annually, with 40 percent of these employees earning less than $20,000 (Statistics Canada 2009a). In contrast, under 1 in 20, or only 4 percent, of workers had incomes of over $100,000. It would be safe to say, then, that while Canadian workers' wages may indeed have been on the rise between 2004 and 2007, a large proportion of Canadians work long hours for relatively low wages, at a time of rising prices and debt loads.

Rising costs and debt loads

Canadian households spent an average of $69,950 in 2007, with most of this spending on personal taxes (21 percent), shelter (20 percent), transportation (13 percent), and food (10 percent). A growing proportion of Canadian households—24.9 percent in 2006—spent 30 percent or more of their income on shelter. Between 2001 and 2006, median annual shelter costs for renters rose 12.8 percent. In general, between 2006 and 2007, Canadian households spent 6 percent more on personal taxes, 5.1 percent more on shelter, 10.6 percent more in mortgage payments, 1.7 percent more on transportation, 6.9 percent more on gasoline, and 3.7 percent more on food—"the fastest annual increase in this category since 2002" (Statistics Canada 2008b; Statistics Canada 2008d). As prices increased, wages clearly did not keep pace. Average household savings have fallen, and average personal and household savings rates reflect this (Sauvé 2008; see Figure 5-5).

Given that Canadian families had a median after-tax income of $58,300 in 2006 (Statistics Canada 2008c; see Table 5-1), their debt loads increased by about 40 percent since 1999 as a direct result. Single-parent families and families headed by someone under the age of 35 carried the highest debt loads in Canada (Statistics Canada 2006b). Not surprising, a Vanier

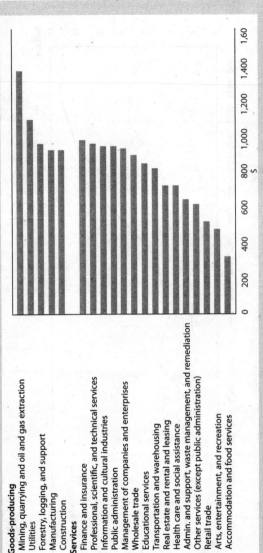

Figure 5-4: Average Weekly Earnings, by Industry, 2007

Source: Statistics Canada 2009a

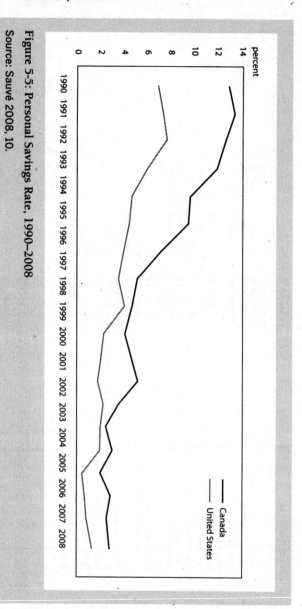

Figure 5-5: Personal Savings Rate, 1990–2008
Source: Sauvé 2008, 10.

Institute of the Family report confirms that debt stress is hardest on lower income households (Sauvé 2008).

Despite rising debt loads, the median net worth of Canadian families increased 23.2 percent between 1999 and 2005. Of those families, those in the top 20 percent of the wealth distribution had a median net worth of about $862,900 in 2005, up 28.5 percent from 1999; they also held 69.2 percent of all personal wealth in the country. In contrast, the 20 percent of families that made up the lowest end of the net worth scale had a median value of $1,000—amounting to a 9.1 percent decline since 1999. The 20 percent of families that made up the bottom of the wealth ladder saw a 2.4 percent increase in

Table 5-1 Family Median After-Tax Income and After-Tax Child Poverty Rate, 2005–2006

	Median Income*	After-tax Child Poverty Rate** 2005	After-tax Child Poverty Rate** 2006	Poverty Difference 2005–2006
Canada	$58,300	11.7%	11.3%	-0.4%
Newfoundland and Labrador	$45,800	10.8%	9.3%	-1.5%
Prince Edward Island	$50,000	3.3%	4.0%	+0.7%
Nova Scotia	$51,600	10.4%	8.7%	-1.7%
New Brunswick	$47,600	10.3%	11.3%	+1.0%
Quebec	$51,500	9.6%	9.7%	+0.1%
Ontario	$62,400	12.6%	11.8%	-0.8%
Manitoba	$53,900	14.1%	12.4%	-1.7%
Saskatchewan	$55,900	12.9%	14.4%	+1.5%
Alberta	$70,500	8.6%	6.9%	-1.7%
British Columbia	$60,300	15.2%	16.1%	+0.9%

Sources:
*Adapted from: Statistics Canada 2008c
**Source: Campaign 2000 2008

their debt load for every $100 of assets, while the debt load for those in the top 20 percent grew at a slower pace (1.6 percent). It would not be inaccurate to conclude that Canada's rich are getting richer and poor are getting poorer, given that families with an after-tax income of $75,000 or more had a net worth of $505,700, up 15.2 percent since 1999, while families whose after-tax income ranged between $20,000 and $29,000 saw a 21.2 percent decline in their median net worth over the same period (Statistics Canada 2006b).

Conclusion

Children are poor for a large number of reasons, but principally due to their parents' relationship to the Canadian labour force, the wages they receive, and the high cost of housing and living. A growing proportion of Canadians are losing jobs in the often well-paid, unionized manufacturing sector, and finding employment in the service sector of the economy. Many of the jobs in Canada's new service economy are lower paid, non-unionized, and often in retail sales. As a result, some Canadian children are poor because their parents earn low wages and/or work at non-standard jobs; others have parents whose education limits them or whose educational credentials are not recognized in Canada, leaving them to face high levels of unemployment or underemployment.

Family earnings instability and inequality has grown throughout the past few decades (Morissette and Ostrovsky 2005). There was, and continues to be, widespread worker displacement and increased worker alienation (Krahn and Lowe 2002; Menzies 2000; Silver, Shields, and Wilson 2005; White 2003). Furthermore, part-time and casual labourers, who are often women, are experiencing increased stress levels, and other physical and emotional problems due to work conditions (Zeytinoglu et al. 2005). It can be concluded that Canada has had and continues to have intolerably high child poverty rates as a result.

Table 5-1 reveals considerable variation in income across provinces. But it is important to note that the wealthiest provinces are not necessarily the ones with the lowest child poverty rates. This tells us that income alone is not enough to understand the root causes of this problem. Social and public policies also play a key role in shaping trends in child poverty. The role of policy will be considered in the next chapter.

Chapter 6

Exploring Causes III
Canada's Changing and Unchanging Policies

As outlined in the previous chapter, Canada's wealthiest provinces are not necessarily the ones with the lowest child poverty rates. In this chapter, we will see that not all economic patterns, trends, and labour-force experiences are the result of global economic factors outside the control of individual governments. Some families find themselves living in or out of poverty because of government decisions and policy shifts. Here, we turn to national and provincial policy decisions that have gone a long way to perpetuate and maintain high rates of poverty, despite the 1989 all-party House of Commons commitment to abolish child poverty by the year 2000. We will review the state of Canada's social safety net and the income security system supposedly in place to protect families from poverty and policy decisions affecting it, as well as consider whether current minimum wages, Employment Insurance (EI), and social assistance benefits are adequate for keeping Canadians with children from living in poverty.

Federal and Provincial Jurisdictions

Canada's political organization has been part of the problem in seriously tackling child poverty in Canada. Canada is a federation of provinces and territories, whereby the federal government in Ottawa is responsible for the development and maintenance of the national body through its control of foreign policy, defence, citizenship and immigration, currency, trade and commerce, criminal law, and the administration of the lives of Canada's First Nations who are governed by the Indian Act. Since Confederation provinces have retained control of the preservation of regional differences and the functioning of everyday life through their responsibility for education, social services (social welfare), health care, labour regulations and standards (for example, minimum wage), language rights, and the regular administration of the criminal justice system. While there have been efforts to maintain universal, cross-Canada standards, such as in health care, this jurisdictional segmentation has amounted to a patchwork of policies and practices across the country, which have made abolishing child poverty by the year 2000, or by any other year, very challenging.

This breakdown of responsibilities and powers makes implementing Canada-wide reforms very difficult. As a result, there is an assortment of policies that aim to achieve different goals, at different tempos, administered to different sets of people, and in different ways. These "jurisdictional complexities" or "tangled hierarchies" (Mahon 2006) have been identified as part of the problem when implementing uniform and comprehensive policies and programs aimed at assisting children and families, and in fulfilling Canada's international obligations, particularly in regard to children's rights, since the 1980s.

Children Speak Out: "If I Was Prime Minister of Canada"

In May and June 2008, over 60 children, from toddlers to teens, took part in a local Children's Consultations initiative on poverty reduction. The consultations were facilitated by children's mental health workers and included a series of questions on family happiness. One of the questions asked of children was: "If you could be the prime minister of Canada, what would you do or change to make all families happy?"

The children's responses varied widely. They said:

> every family would have a home;
> more money;
> buy the toys and things for play;
> supplies and money for school;
> money for medicine;
> I would donate money to all the people who don't have much money;
> buy food and clothing;
> buy birthday presents for everyone;
> shelter and warmness and clothes;
> working for $10.00 an hour;
> donate money to kids so they can go to school;
> make gas prices lower;
> stop animal abuse;
> reduce poverty by giving out money;
> build houses for poor people;
> no more smoking;
> make jobs easier;
> give children who don't have a home one;
> ban weapons;
> everyone has health insurance;
> want safe things;
> banish all the bad drugs;
> more organ donations and blood;
> supply sports equipment;
> give money to kids so they can play sports;
> give people free cars;
> give Tim Horton's more money so more kids can go to camp;
> donate books to kids.

Source: Renfrew County Child Poverty Action Network (CPAN) 2008

CAP to CHST

After the Second World War, the federal government, through conditional transfers and cost-sharing initiatives, intervened in a number of provincial jurisdictions to create or expand a number of social programs and create national standards, including the development of a public health care system, which remains under provincial jurisdiction. What resulted was a period of "co-operative federalism," which for a while was effective in overcoming some provincial divides (Warriner and Peach 2007).[1]

To address increasingly serious concerns about rising poverty throughout 1960s as part of his "war on poverty," in 1966 Prime Minster Lester B. Pearson introduced the Canada Assistance Plan (CAP). CAP was intended to help provinces improve social assistance coverage, support the working poor, and increase access to training. Through CAP federal and provincial governments were committed to unlimited 50:50 cost-sharing for health care, education, and welfare—placing no maximum on the allowable costs incurred (see Little forthcoming; Raphael 2007). It involved the creation of national guidelines for these programs, such as banning the introduction of workfare in Canada, and stressed the principle that welfare was a right to Canadians in economic need. As part of this, there was a relaxation of rules for accessing Unemployment Insurance. CAP did this by providing separate "envelopes" of federal support for social assistance or welfare, health, and post-secondary education.

CAP solidified the popular belief that the Canadian state should help to improve the socio-economic lives of its citizens. Despite economic and political problems (Little forthcoming), the 1960s and 1970s were considered to be the golden age of the Canadian welfare state (Béland and Myles 2004). By 1990 federal increases in CAP contributions to wealthy provinces—British Columbia, Alberta, and Ontario—were capped at 5 percent, which resulted in budget cuts to social assistance at the provincial level (Raphae 2007; Warriner and Peach 2007).

In 1994 the government embarked on a review and overhaul of our social security system due to overlapping budget reductions and to attempt to increase the effectiveness and efficiency of existing programs. Despite the acknowledgement for the need for reform, there was little consensus among the provinces. The October 1994 Social Security Review Discussion Paper outlined a new approach, which included, among other things, a new emphasis on affordability, cost reduction, limiting expenditures, and deficit reduction (Warriner and Peach 2007). Ironically, it retained a commitment to reducing child poverty, but mostly through targeted measures and supports.

Later that year and into 1995, CAP funding was first capped, and then scrapped—replaced by block funding to the provinces, with a continued commitment to improving child benefits. When CAP ended in 1995, so did national standards of social assistance and the prohibition of workfare programs. The Canada Health and Social Transfer (CHST), which replaced CAP as the vehicle for transferring federal funds to the provinces, reduced funding to the provinces, leading to increased restrictions on eligibility (Scott 1998).

As noted above, the CHST was a new structure of federal–provincial fiscal transfers that combined CAP transfers for welfare and social services with health and post-secondary education into a single block of funding. It reduced federal transfers to the provinces by about 7.3 billion over the next three years. In 1995 alone, the CHST resulted in a 15 percent cut to federal transfers for health, post-secondary education, and social assistance (Scott 1998). With the reduction, provinces were given more flexibility and were no longer subject to federal expenditure rules, under the claim that this would make provinces able to pursue innovative approaches to social security reform and effectively shifting responsibility for social programming to provincial hands (see Warriner and Peach 2007). This resulted in lower levels of funding and the elimination of some important standards for social assistance and service provision. CHST ushered in new restrictive eligibility rules on the receipt of Unemployment Insurance, reducing the number of those eligible for benefits.

As this happened, Canada's social safety net became threadbare. Efforts to support workers and families through access to health care, education, community services, and welfare were scaled back (Little forthcoming). This policy shift away from co-operative federalism coincided with a tidal wave of neo-liberal reforms that included a move away from a more universal, social-insurance, rights-based approach, "toward a more targeted, welfare, individualist, needs-tested approach" (Little and Morrison 1999; Warriner and Peach 2007, 47).

The shifting tax burden

As government debt grew throughout the 1980s, some of this debt was the result of increased government spending on financial aid, income transfers, and tax concessions to corporations operating in Canada ($18 billion in 1984). At the same time, federal and provincial governments introduced cost-reduction measures that significantly cut funding to social programs. After the 1970s, there were also changes to the income tax system, which reduced the number of tax brackets from ten to three, decreasing the tax burden of those in the highest tax brackets at the expense of those in the middle and bottom of the income hierarchy. Throughout this period, a growing proportion of federal revenue came from personal income tax—from 26 percent in 1951 to over 50 percent in 1991—while the share from corporate income tax declined—from over 40 percent in 1951 to under 30 percent in 1991 (Warriner and Peach 2007). The addition of the GST also disproportionately disadvantaged low-income earners. This came at a time when Canadians were hit by recessions and by a growing need for social assistance and income support. They received less, rather than more.

From Unemployment Insurance to Employment Insurance

Unemployment Insurance (UI), which is under federal government jurisdiction, was established in 1940 to help offset lost earnings by employees experiencing temporary and infrequent employment. All employed Canadians, employers, and the federal government paid into the federal unemployment insurance system, which in turn allowed most workers to draw weekly benefits—67 percent of their weekly earnings in 1971. Today, employees who become unemployed are eligible for as much as 55 percent of their weekly earnings prior to becoming unemployed (see Table 6-1). It expanded

Table 6-1   Evolution of Unemployment Insurance since 1971

Year	Significant Changes
1971	• The 1971 UI Act is passed • Coverage is extended to virtually all employees • Replacement rate increases to 67% • Benefit durations increase
1977	• Minimum weeks of work needed to claim UI is increased from 8 to 10–14 weeks, depending on the local unemployment rate
1979	• Replacement rate is lowered to 60% • New entrants to the labour market and repeat claimants are required to have more weeks to qualify
1990	• Entrance requirements increase to 10–20 weeks • Benefits durations are reduced
1993	• Replacement rate is lowered to 57% • Those who leave their jobs are made ineligible for UI
1994	• Minimum entrance requirement rate is raised to 12 weeks • Benefit durations are reduced (claimant in a low-employment region can receive a maximum of 36 weeks of benefits) • Replacement rate is lowered to 55%; but for low-income claimants with dependents, replacement rate is raised to 60%
1996	• Repeat users have lower replacement rate • Those with high incomes have part of their benefits restricted through the income tax system • Claimants with few hours in their qualifying period receive lower benefits • Low-income claimants with children receive additional supplement • Maximum duration capped at 45 weeks
2000	• Parental leave extended to 50 weeks • Waiting period for individuals laid off and maternity claims eliminated

Source: Brooks and Miljan 2003

to protect virtually all those in the workforce, except the self-employed, by the 1970s (Battle 2009).

By the mid 1980s and into the early 1990s, various federal bodies held the view that the existing UI system undermined the employability of Canadians and was in need of reform (Warriner and Peach 2007). Some of the changes to UI in the 1990s eliminated government financing, decreased benefits especially for repeat claimants, made eligibility more difficult, and increased workers' contributions (see Table 6-1). There was also the redirection of funds from individuals to job training or retraining programs.

The program's name change in 1996 from Unemployment Insurance to Employment Insurance (EI) brought with it decreased protection for workers and shifted costs to workers, employers, and provincial social services. Employees had to work longer in order to qualify when they lost their jobs, payments were lower, and the maximum duration was reduced (Battle 2009). Unemployment coverage has fallen from 83 percent of workers in 1990 to 43 percent in 2008—the lowest ever, with women faring worse than men (Battle 2009; Battle and Torjman 2009; see Figure 6-1).

In 2009 the maximum weekly regular benefit was $447, or a maximum of $22,350, for up to 50 weeks. This is down from $595 in inflation-adjusted terms ($448 in current dollars) in 1995—or about three-quarters of what it was in 1995. Battle and Battle and Torjman reveal that the 2007 maximum average benefit for women ($298) amounted to $13,410, or $4,544 below the after-tax low-income cut-off (LICO) for a metropolitan area of 500,000 or more residents ($17,954). While slightly better, the 2007 maximum average benefit ($360) for men amounted to $16,200, still $1,754 below the comparable after-tax LICO of $17,954 (Battle 2009; Battle and Torjman 2009). With changes to EI, losing one's job in 2007, even when covered by EI at maximum levels (and not all are eligible), has resulted in families living on low income. In 2009 the situation looks bleaker as unemployment rates spiked (see Figure 6-2). People living on social assistance fared no better.

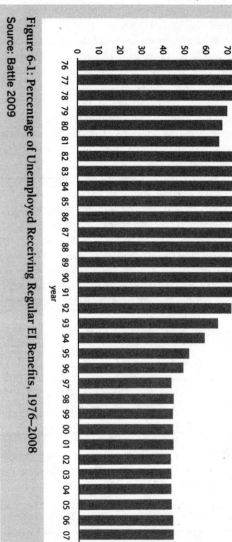

Figure 6-1: Percentage of Unemployed Receiving Regular EI Benefits, 1976–2008

Source: Battle 2009

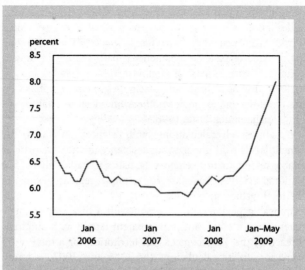

Figure 6-2: Unemployment Rate, 2006–2009
Source: Statistics Canada 2009c

Changes to social assistance

Social assistance, or what is commonly referred to as "welfare"—the social safety net of last resort—falls under provincial jurisdiction. It is made up of a range of programs and services that vary across and within provinces, depending on whether someone is deemed employable or not, single, a single-parent with a child, single with a disability, or part of a two-parent family with children (National Council of Welfare 2008b; Raphael 2007).

In the early 1990s, even before the elimination of CAP and the introduction of CHST, many on social assistance in diverse parts of the country began experiencing reductions in benefits and restrictions in eligibility for benefits. Situations deteriorated with the introduction of CHST. Throughout the first half of the 1990s, Saskatchewan reduced benefits to those deemed employable, New Brunswick restricted access, and Alberta and Ontario cut benefit rates. Some provinces introduced mandatory "workfare," which involves looking for or gaining paid employment or participating in unpaid volunteer work as part of eligibility. (For a detailed look at various provincial programs placing a growing emphasis on the employment of single mothers on social assistance, see Little forthcoming; Little 1998.)

By almost all calculations, and in most provinces, the benefit levels paid under social assistance are not adequate to enable recipients to live above Statistics Canada's LICO. The National Council of Welfare, for example, regularly estimates the total welfare income for four types of households (single employable person, single person with a disability, a single parent with a child, and a two-parent family with children) in each of the 13 provinces and territories, for a total of 53 scenarios. In its calculations for 2006 and 2007, it found that welfare incomes in 2006 were less than two-thirds of the after-tax LICOs for 22 of the 53 scenarios (National Council of Welfare 2008b). The situation was worse in 2007. They found that single parents in Newfoundland and Labrador fared the best, and were closest to the poverty line. In most other provinces families fared worse. In fact, in 2006–2007 welfare incomes were at their lowest point since 1986. So why not try to "get off" welfare?

Some have argued that our income tax system, social assistance benefits, subsidy structure, and current economic climate with growth in low-waged, non-standard jobs (jobs often lacking benefits, and often making workers ineligible for Employment Insurance benefits should they lose their job) discourages the "employable unemployed" on social assistance from seeking work. The reality for many who find paid work is that they end up in low-paying jobs, with few or no benefits, and increased costs for housing, child care, prescription medications, etc. not covered by social assistance or workplace benefits. Because of these circumstances, especially the low wages, many find themselves in a "poverty trap." With low-paying jobs as the best prospect for many on social assistance, it makes little economic sense to try to "get off" welfare. Let us explore in more detail provincial governments' initiatives when it comes to low wages.

Minimum wages

The percentage or proportion of low-waged workers in a country or province is one of the best predictors of poverty in that population (Raphael 2007). The connection between and concern with poverty and low wages is not new. In 1968 a Special Senate Committee on Poverty was established to investigate poverty in Canada. Its 1971 report, *Poverty in Canada*, identified insufficient wages as a major cause of poverty (Smeeding 2005). Around the same time, *The Report of the Royal Commission on the Status of Women* (1970) also expressed concerns about the ongoing link between low wages and poverty.

,Minimum wages are set by the provinces and range widely, from a high of $10.00 per hour in Nunavut to a low of $7.75 in New Brunswick (Canada Online 2009). British Columbia, interestingly, has gone from having one of the highest minimum wages rates ($8.00 in 2004) (Statistics Canada 2005c) only a few years ago, to having among the lowest, as some provinces introduced consecutive increases year over year, surpassing BC.

In 2004, 621,000 Canadians worked at or below the minimum wage, amounting to about 4.6 percent of all employees in Canada (Statistics Canada 2005c). By 2008 that number jumped to 751,400 or 5.2 percent (see Table 6-2). Women were disproportionately more likely to work for minimum wage, and they accounted for 60 percent of all minimum-wage workers, but just under half of all employees (Statistics Canada 2009d). Almost 30 percent of all workers earning minimum wage or less were between the ages of 25 and 54, and minimum-waged work was concentrated in the service sector, with more than one in five workers in the accommodation and food services earning minimum wages or below (Statistics Canada 2009d). By almost all measures, earning minimum wage resulted in individuals and families

Table 6-2 Share of Employees Working for Minimum Wage or Less by Province, 2000–2008

	2000	2001	2002	2003	2004	2005	2006	2007	2008
					%				
Canada	**4.7**	**4.8**	**4.8**	**4.1**	**4.6**	**4.3**	**4.3**	**5.0**	**5.2**
Newfoundland and Labrador	8.7	5.7	7.4	8.4	6.5	6.1	7.6	7.4	7.7
Prince Edward Island	3.7	3.2	4.4	4.0	4.4	5.1	4.7	6.9	5.6
Nova Scotia	4.9	4.1	4.6	5.9	5.6	5.1	5.9	6.2	6.4
New Brunswick	6.0	4.2	4.2	4.1	2.5	3.1	4.1	5.6	4.8
Quebec	5.4	7.0	6.1	5.1	4.4	4.6	4.2	5.4	5.9
Ontario	4.6	4.1	3.9	3.5	5.3	4.3	4.7	6.3	6.6
Manitoba	5.1	4.5	4.8	4.5	4.9	4.9	4.8	5.5	5.3
Saskatchewan	5.9	4.4	4.8	5.0	3.3	3.9	5.4	3.2	3.8
Alberta	2.0	1.5	1.1	1.1	0.9	1.3	1.7	1.0	1.6
British Columbia	4.5	6.0	7.7	5.6	6.2	5.6	4.6	3.4	2.7

Source: Statistics Canada 2009f

living in poverty. Changes to provincial minimum wage legislation, which would substantially raise minimum wages, would go a long way towards helping some Canadians move out of poverty.[2]

Conclusion

Over the past few decades we have been witnessing changing levels of income supports through government transfers across Canada. For some Canadians, their economic circumstances have deteriorated, precisely at a time when Canada's social safety net has become tattered and weak. Since the 1980s we have seen a rise in neo-liberal policies and in cutbacks to the welfare state, resulting in increased polarization between Canada's rich and poor.

Overall, children themselves may be contributing to family poverty because typically they are a drain on family resources. However, research shows that in some countries with more family-friendly social policies, disposable income falls only moderately when families have children. Using data from seven Western, industrialized countries, Sigle-Rushton and Waldfogel (2007) compared gaps in gross and disposable family income between families with and without children. They found that differences in earnings and labour-market participation of women were major reasons for the gap in gross and disposable income. Taxes and government transfers also narrowed the gap in disposable income between families with and without children. On a number of fronts, Canada is comparatively worse than other developed nations in their level of support to families with children. The next chapter considers in more detail how Canada compares to other nations and what accounts for some of the similarities and differences.

Chapter 7

International Comparisons and Accounting for the Differences

The true measure of a nation's standing is how well it attends to its children—their health and safety, their material security, their education and socialization, and their sense of being loved, valued, and included in the families and societies into which they are born.

UNICEF 2007

How Does Canada Compare Internationally?

If the true measure of a nation's standing is how well it treats its children, Canada's standing ranks very low. When using child poverty as a measure for a nation's "treatment" of children, Denmark and Finland sit atop the national standings, with child poverty rates of less than 3 percent. Canada, even in its most prosperous times, lands too shamefully close to the bottom (UNICEF 2005; see Figure 7-1).

In 2005 UNICEF released its *Report Card No. 6—Child Poverty in Rich Countries*. It found that throughout the 1990s, the proportion of children living in poverty in developed nations increased in 17 out of the 24 Organization for Economic Co-operation and Development (OECD) countries (Corak 2006).[1] While child poverty rates dropped slightly in Canada over the ten years during the investigation (see Figure

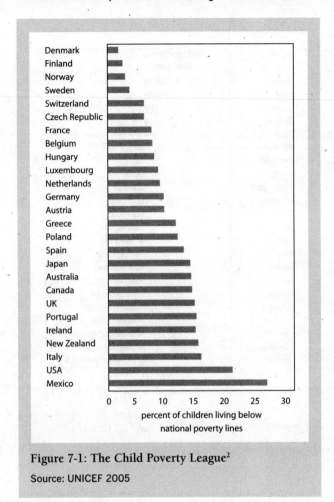

Figure 7-1: The Child Poverty League[2]
Source: UNICEF 2005

7-2), it still ranked 19th out of 26 countries—with 14.9 percent of its children living in poverty. All six non-European countries compared, as well as Canada, were in the bottom half of the scale, with English-speaking countries at the very bottom. For example, the country immediately above Canada was Australia (number 18 of 26), and below Canada were the

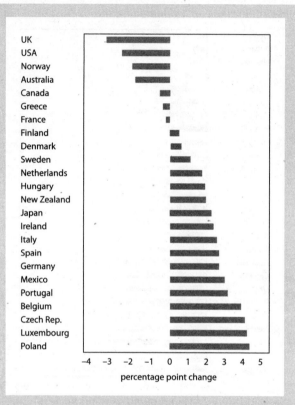

Figure 7-2: Changes in Child Poverty Rates, 1990s
Source: UNICEF 2005

UK,[3] Portugal, Ireland, New Zealand, Italy, the United States, and Mexico (UNICEF 2005).

The same report found that while labour market conditions and social change played key roles in high child poverty rates, higher government spending on, and better distribution of, family and social benefits are clearly associated with lower child poverty rates. The report noted that in all countries, poverty levels are determined by a combination of three forces: social trends, labour market conditions, and government policies (UNICEF 2005)—as we have seen in Chapters 4, 5, and 6 of this book.[4] How does Canada compare on these three forces at the international level?

Labour Market Shifts and Trends: How We Are Similar

Canada is very similar to many other developed nations, and at the same time very different. To begin with, Canada was swept up in the same post–Second World War global economic trends as other industrialized nations. Between the 1940s and 1960s, like the governments of these other nations, the Canadian government was actively involved in establishing and supporting economic regulation *and* social programs, including the expansion of welfare benefits, Unemployment Insurance, public health care, and retirement insurance. This period of social and economic "prosperity" was followed by significant international shifts.

For most economically developed nations, including Canada, the 1970s ushered in global economic deregulation and restructuring, as well as the rise of neo-liberalism, international trade liberalization, and market integration—making it easier for corporations to move production to where labour and other resources were cheaper and more plentiful. There was increased economic competition and pressures to cut costs, including labour costs, and to maximize profits. Governments intervened more to enhance productivity and competitiveness, and less to protect workers and living standards. Freer trade and corporate mobility resulted in the deterioration of employment income, labour standards, social welfare, and environmental protection (Warriner and Peach 2007).

Despite their significant public support, social policy initiatives put in place during and immediately following the Second World War to address some of the detrimental effects of economic restructuring came under strain and attack throughout the 1980s and 1990s. This was as true for Canada as it was for many other industrialized nations around the world. In contrast, for the past 20 years the Nordic countries—Sweden, Finland, Norway, and Denmark—have held child poverty rates at about 5 percent, even during the early 1990s when their economies were weak, and unemployment was rising (Kamerman et al. 2003). The same cannot be said for Canada, even as employment rates stabilized and improved.

Both Canada and the US, for example, had major job losses in manufacturing, with declines deeper and longer in the US than in Canada. US manufacturing employment dropped sharply by 21 percent between 1998 and 2007, while Canada registered a decline of 12 percent from 2000 to 2007. Though manufacturing employment declined between 2000 and 2007, Canada's employment growth was stronger than that of the US in construction, trade, mining, oil and gas, utilities, business services, and public administration (Statistics Canada 2009a). Compared to the US and various other nations, Canada fared relatively well—but poverty rates remained high.

Between 1997 and 2007, Canada's employment rate increased by 4.6 percent. Sweden, Australia, and Italy had similar increases. The Netherlands saw the biggest increase in its employment rate, 6.1 percent, while Germany, the United Kingdom, and France all saw rises of 1 to 3 percent. Employment rates fell in Japan (–3.4 percent) and also in the US (–0.8 percent) during this 10-year period. Canada posted healthy employment gains, and for the past five years a higher proportion of women were working in Canada than in any of these countries, reaching an employment rate of 59.7 percent in 2007 (Statistics Canada 2009a).

In light of this economic "prosperity," and in the midst of dramatic economic change, it would seem likely that Canada's child poverty rates would be lower than those in many other industrialized nations, but this is not the case. Despite all this, Canada still ranked 19 out of 26 countries compared (UNICEF 2005). It is evident that child poverty rates are affected by something other than labour market conditions

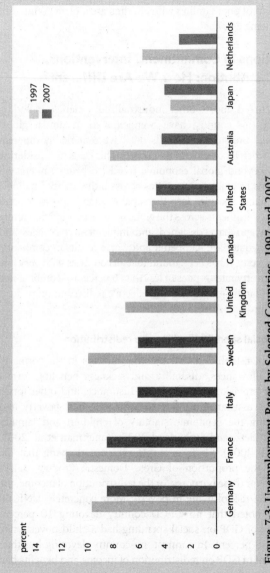

Figure 7-3: Unemployment Rates by Selected Countries, 1997 and 2007

Source: US Department of Labor 2008

alone. After all, on average across OECD countries, only about one-third of poor families with children are jobless (Whiteford and Adema 2007).

Variations in Commitment, Interventions, and Distribution: How We Are Different

As discussed above, other industrialized societies, including parts of this country, have been exposed to similar global economic pressures and shifts but have remarkably different results when it comes to child poverty. This leads to considering factors beyond global economic trends to better understand variations in child poverty rates across industrialized nations. While many societies face the same economic pressures and shifts, governments across the globe have responded differently to them and have designed and implemented policies and programs that have had better and worse results in combating child poverty. It has been found that all countries with very low child poverty rates—rates of less than 5 percent—combine low levels of family joblessness and effective redistribution policies (Whiteford and Adema 2007).

More social spending and income redistribution

It is well established that income transfers in the forms of family allowances, disability and sickness benefits, formal daycare provisions, Employment Insurance, and other forms of social assistance are key to reducing child poverty and enhancing the economic stability of children and families (Corak, Lietz, and Sutherland 2005; Kamerman et al. 2003; UNICEF 2005). There is ample evidence showing that the greater the proportion of Gross Domestic Product (GDP) devoted for these purposes, or the redistribution of income, the lower the risk of living in poverty. More concretely, UNICEF (2005) noted that no OECD country devoting 10 percent or more of GDP on social spending had a child poverty rate above 10 percent. In contrast, no country devoting less than 5 percent of GDP on redistribution of income and benefits had a child poverty rate of less than 15 percent (UNICEF 2005; see Figure 7-4). Differences in social transfers and social spending have amounted to some countries reducing child poverty by as much as 20 percent, while other countries by as little as 5 percent. These economic benefits to families have significantly and successfully protected children from poverty in Austria, Belgium, France, the Netherlands, and the UK, while in Ireland, Italy, Greece, Portugal, and Spain benefits have been low, resulting in higher than average poverty rates (Kamerman et al. 2003). According to a UNICEF (2000) study, taxes and social transfers have reduced child poverty in France from 28.7 percent to 7.9 percent. In contrast, in Italy, taxes push two-parent families further into poverty than transfers help to lift them out (Kamerman et al. 2003). Not surprising given its high child poverty rate, Canada was among one of the few countries that actually *decreased* its share of social spending

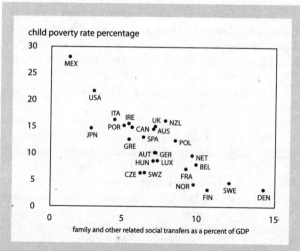

Figure 7-4: Social Transfers Relating to Family Economic Security

Source: UNICEF 2005

between 1990 and 2000 (UNICEF 2005). However, many have added that income or social transfers alone are insufficient to eliminate child poverty.

Not just "how much?" but also "how?"

UNICEF's report card on child poverty shows that all the nations studied made significant efforts to reduce levels of poverty through cash and other benefits to the unemployed and those living on low income. However, countries with the world's lowest rates of poverty, such as Denmark, Finland, and Norway, did a considerably better job in regard to government intervention. As noted above, the study found that the greater the proportion of GDP devoted to family allowances, disability and sickness benefits, formal daycare provisions, Employment Insurance, employment promotion, and other forms of social assistance, the lower the risk of growing up in poverty (UNICEF 2005). On top of how much was spent, it was also important to factor in how government support was distributed (Whiteford and Adema 2007). For example, in France the taxes and benefits system does not favour any particular age group, or is it aimed specifically at reducing poverty. Instead, child poverty rates are low because of a mix of universal and targeted programs that prevent and protect a large number of children and families from poverty (Kamerman et al. 2003).

The UNICEF (2005) report, like many others, explained that when benefits are universally provided—provided to everyone, rather than aimed at low-income families—though seemingly more expensive, actually work best. Highly targeted (means-tested) social expenditures—as is commonly the case in the US and Canada—focus resources on those who need it most, but may mean that recipients have little incentive to move from welfare to often low-skilled, low-waged work (Kamerman et al. 2003; UNICEF 2005). Means-tested programs have also proven to be inefficient, highly ineffective, and stigmatizing.

Corak, Lietz, and Sutherland (2005) assessed the impact of tax and transfer systems on children and child poverty rates in the European Union (EU) and found that countries with the lowest child poverty rates were those in which children benefited from social transfers not necessarily directed at them—but rather directed at supporting their working parent or parents. These countries also had universal benefits and tax concessions that did not target low-income children and families. Children benefited most from universal programs that protect them and their families from becoming poor in the first place. Countries with targeted programs had levels of spending comparable to other nations, but child poverty rates were higher (Corak, Lietz, and Sutherland 2005).

Canada has made efforts to reduce poverty; however, initiatives consisted of a tattered patchwork of policies and targeted programs and not a unified and comprehensive poverty reduction strategy or system—as is the case in European nations with low or rapidly declining child poverty rates. Take the United Kingdom, for example. For most of the 1990s and into 2000, it had high child poverty rates— comparable to or worse than Canada's poverty rate at that time. Since 1999, and especially since 2005, the UK has been implementing a poverty reduction strategy that is focused and goal-oriented: to reduce poverty by 25 percent by 2005; by 50 percent by 2010; and to eradicate completely by 2020. This strategy is also multi-pronged: it included the enactment of a number of laws (e.g., Welfare Reform Act 2007, Equality Act 2006, and Childcare Act 2006) and the implementation of a wide range of initiatives in partnership with the community sector (Collin 2007b).

The UK's multi-pronged approach emerged from the recognition that there was a range of factors contributing to poverty: a lack of education and training, low labour market participation, poor work conditions, a lack of affordable housing, a lack of accessible public transport systems, poor health, high rates of crime, and a need for better access to affordable, high-quality child care (Collin 2007b). To reduce poverty and promote social inclusion, the government introduced changes to the taxation system, established a national minimum wage, as well as tax credits for low-income

Millions of UK Young in Poverty

BBC News, 30 September 2008

The Campaign to End Child Poverty says 5.5 million children are in families that are classed as "struggling"—98% of children in some areas.

The campaign classes households as being in poverty if they are living on under £10 per person per day.

A government spokeswoman said it had lifted 600,000 children out of poverty and was committed to the cause.

The Campaign to End Child Poverty is a coalition of more than 130 organisations including Barnardo's, UNICEF and the NSPCC.

According to its research, there are 4,634,000 children in England living in low income families, 297,000 in Wales, 428,000 in Scotland and 198,000 in Northern Ireland.

It says 174 of the 646 parliamentary constituencies in Britain have 50% or more of their child population in, or close to, the poverty line.

The parliamentary constituency with the highest number of children in or close to poverty is Birmingham Ladywood, with 81% (28,420 individuals).

Campaign director Hilary Fisher said the figures were "absolutely shocking."

She said: "There are currently 3,900,000 children in the UK that are classed as actually living in poverty, which impacts on every aspect of a child's life.

"A child in poverty is 10 times more likely to die in infancy, and five times more likely to die in an accident.

"Adults who lived in poverty as a child are 50 times more likely to develop a restrictive illness such diabetes or bronchitis."

Ms Fisher said some families could not afford school uniforms, and chose schools for their children based on uniform cost—which was "not acceptable."

She said: "The government has lifted 600,000 children out of poverty, but 100,000 have gone back for each of the last two years.

"If the government does not allocate £3bn in tax credits and benefits in the next budget, then their plans to reduce child poverty will fail."

A spokeswoman for the Department for Children, Schools and Families said the government was committed to the cause.

She said: "We have lifted 600,000 children out of poverty, we are introducing free nursery education for all two, three and four year olds and have seen an increase in educational outcomes at all ages."

She said local authorities and other service providers had to help it raise family incomes, encourage people to apply for tax credit and benefits and help parents work.

She said the latter was known to be one of the best ways for families to get out of poverty

Donald Hirsch, author of several reports on child poverty, said a single-wage couple with two children would stop getting Working Tax Credit when they were on £18,500 a year—leaving them just above the poverty line.

He said: "The official government measure of poverty is families below 60% of median income before housing costs, so families with this composition on Working Tax Credit will be close to the poverty line."

The report's figures are made up from Child Tax Credit and Working Tax Credit data, and have been calculated by the Centre for Economic and Social Inclusion.

Another area with high child poverty is Bethnal Green and Bow, which has 79% (23,450) of its children in low income families.

The constituency of Bradford West has 75% (24,900) of children in or near poverty, while Nottingham East has 68% (12,360).

Government pledge

An estimated 98% of children living in two zones in Glasgow Baillieston—Central Easterhouse and North Barlarnark and Easterhouse South—are either in poverty or in working families that are "struggling to get by."

And there are 58% of children in Swansea East (10,470) in families of this description.

The constituencies with the lowest levels of families in, or near, poverty are Buckingham and Sheffield Hallam, both with 17%.

At last week's Labour Party conference, Prime Minister Gordon Brown said child poverty "demeans Britain" and repeated his party's pledge to halve child poverty by 2010, and ultimately to end it.

During his speech he said: "The measures we have taken this year alone will help lift 250,000 children out of poverty.

"The economic times are tough—of course that makes things harder—but we are in this for the long haul. The complete elimination of child poverty by 2020."

Harry Potter author JK Rowling recently donated £1m to the Labour Party, saying she was motivated by Labour's record on child poverty.

But shadow work and pensions secretary Chris Grayling said the figures "underline the vast social divide" within cities.

'Broken Britain'

He added: "There are examples of wards within cities where hardly any children live in poverty but sitting alongside these wards are others where virtually every family lives below the poverty line.

"This just goes to show the extent to which Britain is truly broken."

The Scottish government said it was helping low-income families with a council tax freeze, abolishing prescription charges and piloting free school meals.

"However, the limited nature of devolved powers restricts our ability to act," a spokesman said.

"We need significant extra investment by the UK government."

The report's results are for the period of August 2006, except for ward or zone breakdowns, which are for August 2005.

The Campaign to End Child Poverty will stage a rally in London's Trafalgar Square on Saturday 4 October called Keep The Promise, where it will call on Gordon Brown to keep Labour's promises on child poverty.

Source: Brighton 2008

earners and tax credits and measures to support parents, seniors, and people with disabilities (Collin 2007b). It also significantly increased spending on education, employment assistance, health care, and housing. The UK is not alone in the creation of a national, comprehensive poverty reduction strategy. Canada, on the other hand, continues to lag behind.

The National Council of Welfare assessed anti-poverty strategies in other countries and found that the EU framework contained objectives that Canada could learn from and model. One of the most obvious was that it promoted social cohesion, equality between men and women, interaction among policies, transparency, good governance, and the monitoring of policy. Especially effective within the EU framework was that it did not isolate the problem of poverty but instead viewed it as connected to larger economic, social, and political issues (National Council of Welfare 2007g). Having this larger perspective, followed by more comprehensive and unified initiatives, is more closely connected to a specific policy approach—an approach not shared by countries like Canada and the United States.

Differing policy regimes

In contrast to national, unified, and comprehensive poverty reduction strategies just identified, the mixture of Canadian policies (mostly targeted or means-tested), like those in the US, assume and reflect the perspective that a main cause of poverty is the individual and his or her personal choices and actions. From this starting point, it is clear why an "individual responsibility" model, or framework to social or family policy, is embraced. This approach to the understanding and treatment of families does not recognize society's shared responsibility for children (Freiler and Cerny 1998). This perspective assumes that having children is an individual lifestyle choice and the responsibility of those who choose to have them. The state will step in to assist families, but only after they find themselves in dire need. In contrast, most Western European nations with low poverty rates embrace a "social responsibility" or social democratic framework that assumes that children are essential to the society, and as such are the responsibility both of parents *and* of the state. They have more unified social and family programs and policies that express society's shared responsibility for children, provide an adequate income floor for families with children, reduce gender inequalities, expand family time options for parents, and ensure an adequate and consistent living standard for all children and families (Freiler and Cerny 1998). Canada, like the US, is very far from embracing such a framework.[5]

Canada is a welfare state: the federal, provincial and territorial governments, and civil service accept some responsibility for the protection and promotion of the economic and social well-being of its citizens, through things like Employment Insurance, access to basic health care and education, etc. But not all welfare states are alike. In fact, policy scholars have examined welfare states and have distinguished them as "more generous," "less generous," and "laissez-faire." Laissez-faire welfare states have less government investment and support. Canada, like the US, has been classified as a liberal welfare state, which means that it is among the "less generous," relying on the free market rather than extensive state support to families and social programs (Esping-Andersen 1990; 2007). Within liberal welfare states, there is a shared basic assumption that the state will step in if citizens are in dire need, often with targeted rather than universal social programs. Otherwise the state leaves social welfare decisions to individuals.

Canada relies heavily on income-tested and needs-tested (not universal) programs such as social assistance. Social assistance schemes or programs in liberal welfare states typically have strict entitlement regulations, with modest and short-tem benefits. These contribute to higher than average child poverty rates. Given that there are "more generous" or social democratic variations of welfare states, not all countries follow this liberal model or agree with its basic premises.

Social democratic regimes are more likely to implement universal programs—or programs available to people from different age groups, walks of life, and socio-economic backgrounds. Social democratic regimes are more likely to support programs promoting the material, educational, emotional, and physical well-being of all its citizens—to prevent poverty (see UNICEF 2007 for national comparisons). This is done through the implementation of generous parental or maternity leaves, paid health and family related leaves, employment supports, accessible child care programs, national housing strategies, etc. (Heymann, Barrera, and Earle 2008). They are significantly less likely than liberal regimes, like Canada, to foster the precedence of the market when it comes to the well-being of its citizens.

Conclusion

While many countries find themselves in a similar economic situation as Canada, their child poverty rates are not comparable. Some of the difference in child poverty rates has to do with *how much* nations spend on social programs; but more importantly, differences can be attributed to *how* resources are redistributed and the social policies and policy paradigms that underlie them.

UNICEF's (2005) report card noted that higher government spending on family and other social benefits was associated with lower child poverty rates. But it also reported that among countries with roughly similar levels of government spending, child poverty rates varied from between 3 and 15 percent. They explained that child poverty rates are likely not only a function of *levels* of government spending, but of *distribution* as well. They concluded that "many OECD countries would appear to have the potential to reduce child poverty below 10 percent without a significant increase in overall spending" (UNICEF 2005, 5).

In Canada we do not have to look very far for initiatives that resemble unified, comprehensive, and social democratic policy models. For approximately the last ten years, Quebec has been unfolding components of a family policy unparalleled in North America, aimed at reconciling work and family, promoting gender equity, and reducing family poverty (Roy and Bernier 2007; see Chapter 8). Through a number of initiatives, Quebec has demonstrated to the rest of Canada that combating child poverty is not impossible or out of reach. This also highlights the importance of creating a unified national strategy that recognizes poverty as linked to larger economic, social, and political issues and decisions. More specifically, fighting poverty would require the creation of a better, more integrated system of income supports and services aimed at helping a larger number of Canadians and families, and preventing people from falling into poverty in the first place. The next chapter will present a number of recommendations and options for Canada.

Chapter 8

Solutions Proposed and Tested and Recommendations for Change

In 1989 the child poverty rate in Canada was about 12 percent—the same as it was in 2007. While we celebrated the drop to 12 percent in 2007, the rate of 12 percent in 1989 was considered cause for alarm and shame. Times have changed, and yet some things have not.

In 1989 Canada was viewed as a "social policy laggard" (Freiler and Cerny 1998), meaning that compared to the rest of the industrialized world, Canada fell far behind other countries in providing social and economic benefits to Canadian families—particularly to those with young children. Shamed into attention, on 24 November 1989, the House of Commons unanimously passed an all-party resolution to eliminate poverty among Canadian children by the year 2000. All parties seemed to have agreed that 12 percent of Canada's children living in poverty was not acceptable, and should be reduced and then eliminated.[1]

The next year, in 1990, at the World Summit for Children, Canada reaffirmed its commitment by agreeing to the principle of "first call for children"—that the basic needs of children would be a priority in the allocation of resources (UNICEF 1990b). One year later, in 1991, Canada ratified the UN Convention on the Rights of the Child. In doing this, the federal government agreed to implement measures—to the "maximum extent" of its resources—to fulfill, among others, article 27: "The right of every child to a standard of living adequate for the child's physical, mental, spiritual, moral and social development." In 2000 Canada, along with 188 other members of the United Nations, made another commitment to eliminate extreme poverty, a commitment made in the context of the Millennium Development Goals (Heyman, Barrera, and Earle 2008). On paper, Canada seemed fully committed to addressing child poverty, with public pledges made at home and abroad. The federal government's actions, though, were weak and far less concrete. It did, however, implement changes to child benefits to attempt to reduce high child poverty rates (see Table 8-1).

Since the 1989 commitment, the federal government revamped the child benefits system. By 1993 the three federal child benefits that reached (or intended to reach) all families with children—the Family Allowance, the Refundable Child Tax Credit, and the Nonrefundable Child Tax Credit—were replaced by the income tested Canada Child Tax Benefit (CCTB) based on how much income a family earns. This initiative increased benefits for working-poor families with children, maintained benefits for low-income families, reduced benefits for middle-income earners, and eliminated benefits for high-income families (Battle 2007). Despite these benefits, child poverty rates skyrocketed throughout the early 1990s. In 1995 there were about 1,472,000 children, or 21 percent of all children, living in low-income families (Statistics Canada 1996). This was an increase of 538,000 children, or 58 percent, since 1989—the year the House of Commons made its commitment to eliminate child poverty by the year 2000 (Freiler and Cerny 1998). In 1989 one child in seven was poor. In 1999 almost one in five was poor (Campaign 2000 2002).

In 1998 the federal, provincial, and territorial governments enacted more profound changes by introducing the National Child Benefit (NCB) Supplement.[2] This restructured and attempted to coordinate various child benefits at the two

Table 8-1 The History of Child Benefits in Canada

1918	Child Tax Exemption: This exemption provided income tax savings that increased as taxable income increased. It did not provide benefits to families that did not have a tax liability.
1945	Family Allowance: This benefit was provided to all Canadian families with dependent children.
1973	The Family Allowance benefits were tripled, indexed to the cost of living, and made taxable.
1978	Refundable Child Tax Credit: This targeted and income-tested child benefit, which was delivered through the tax system, provided a maximum benefit to low-income families, a declining amount to middle-income families, and no benefit to upper-income families.
1993	Child Tax Benefit (CTB): This benefit consolidated refundable and non-refundable child tax credits and the Family Allowance into a monthly payment based on the number of children and level of family income. It also included the Working Income Supplement (WIS), which provided an additional benefit to low-income working families with children. In 1993, federal expenditures on child benefits, including WIS, totalled $5.1 billion.
1998	The CTB was replaced by the Canada Child Tax Benefit (CCTB). The National Child Benefit (NCB) Supplement replaced the WIS, and is provided to all low-income families as part of the new CCTB.
2006	The Government of Canada introduced the Universal Child Care Benefit (UCCB). All families, including low-income families, receive $100 a month for each child under the age of six, taxable in the hands of the lower-income spouse.
2007	Budget 2007 announced a new Child Tax Credit which provides additional tax relief for families with children. For 2007, this tax credit provides up to $306 in tax savings for each child under the age of 18.

Source: Government of Canada 2008

levels of government through the income-tested CCTB and the NCB Supplement (see Figure 8-1). The goals were to help prevent and reduce child poverty, promote parental attachment to the labour force, and reduce overlap and duplication by harmonizing programs through a simplified administration (Government of Canada 2007). The federal–provincial/territorial agreement was implemented based on the understanding that as Ottawa increased payments under the CCTB to working and non-working poor families, the provinces and territories could reduce social-assistance-related child benefits. This was supposed to free up provincial and territorial funds for reinvestment into other programs and services for low-income families with children (Battle 2007). It amounted to a claw back of funds in some provinces.[3] The federal and provincial/territorial governments estimated that $2,500 as an average amount per child was required for the new CCTB to displace most social assistance-provided child benefits in most provinces (Mendelson 2005). It was expected that all low-income families with children, whether working or non-working, would receive more federal funding, while families on social assistance would still benefit from some provincially funded social welfare programs.

National child benefits have been effective in reducing poverty—without federal child benefits, the number of low-income families with children would almost double—but the number of children in poverty would be significantly reduced by further increases (up to $5,000) to the CCTB (Battle 2007, 2008; Battle and Torjman 2009).[4] Some have argued the CCTB and NCB Supplement have been effective in closing the poverty gap; however, they do very little to address the issue of unemployment and low employment earnings which contribute to family poverty in the first place (Mendelson 2005). Mendelson notes that child benefits should ideally be large enough to eliminate poverty (through the redistribution of resources), and also should work in combination with efforts to improve adult income from and through employment, training allowances, and other income security programs. Until then, our child poverty rates will remain high in comparison with other Organization for Economic Co-operation and Development (OECD) countries. Much more needs to be done.

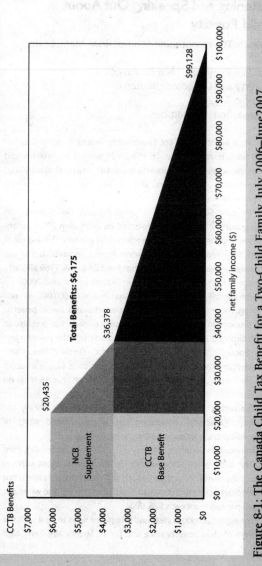

Figure 8-1: The Canada Child Tax Benefit for a Two-Child Family, July 2006–June2007
Source: Government of Canada 2008

Listening and Speaking Out About Child Poverty

Speech: The Honourable Senator Rose-Marie Losier-Cool
Acadian Peninsula, New Brunswick
Poverty and Canadian children
October 17, 2007
Ottawa, Senate Chamber

Hon. Rose-Marie Losier Cool: Honourable senators, today, October 17, is the International Day for the Eradication of Poverty. I would like to speak briefly about poverty in Canada, and particularly about children living in poverty and also parents, since poor children do not come from rich parents.

This past September 11, a comprehensive policy report on child poverty in Canada was released by Campaign 2000, a non-partisan network dedicated to ending child poverty. The author of the 48-page report, Professor Marvyn Novick, reminds us that we, as federal parliamentarians, have not lived up to our 1989 all-party promise to eliminate child poverty in Canada by the year 2000.

Honourable senators, still today, in 2007, 800,000 of our children, more than one out of every ten children, live in poverty. This proportion has not changed since we made the promise in 1989, almost 20 years ago. Statistics Canada sets the poverty line at an annual income of less than $27,000 for a family of four. I think we can agree that that is not much to feed, clothe, house, educate and transport four people — sometimes difficult choices must be made.

The report examines the prevalence of poverty among our children, especially considering the unprecedented years of economic prosperity our country is experiencing.

Honourable senators, why must our children be hungry, cold and left aside when our country's Human Development Index is sixth in the world? Why does Canada still have poor kids when our gross domestic product is ranked eighth in the world and when our wealth per capita exceeds $28, 000?

The report proposes clear and integrated ways to deal with the problem of child poverty once and for all. Specifically, Campaign

2000 recommends that child poverty in Canada be reduced by at least 25 per cent by 2012 and by at least 50 per cent by 2017.

To reach this realistic goal, the federal government should up its Child Tax Benefit to $5 100 per year. This increase alone would reduce the rate of child poverty in Canada by 37 per cent. The federal government should also increase its work tax credits.

Federal and provincial governments should guarantee a $10 per hour minimum wage, make substantial investments in early childhood education and childcare, and put more money into social housing.

Furthermore, the provinces should expand their coverage for prescription drugs and dental care and enable families to take full advantage of the federal government's annual child benefit by not clawing it back from social assistance benefits paid to society's poorest families.

Source: Senate of Canada 2007

Simply Not Enough

In 2004 the Senate Human Rights Committee embarked on a study of Canada's international obligations in relation to the rights and freedoms of children. In 2005 it filed an interim report that indicated that the UN's Convention on the Rights of the Child has not been incorporated into Canadian law and that there continue to be large gaps in its implementation. This report was followed by another in 2007 which identified the ongoing shortcomings and inadequacies on the part of the Canadian government when implementing programs aimed at improving children's rights—views echoed by many scholars and activists (Howe and Covell 2007). The Senate committee found that the large gap between "rhetoric and reality" leaves Canadian children vulnerable, with no representation at the federal government level to work on their behalf. In response, the Senate committee called for the implementation of a children's commissioner. The report includes a long list of recommendations on a number of issues, including corporal punishment, bullying, sexual exploitation, child protection, adoption, health, and child poverty (Andreychuk and Fraser 2007).[5] Andreychuk and Fraser's reports and Howe and Covell's work (2003, 2007) remind us that Canada's high child poverty rates are, at the very least, in violation of the UN Convention on the Rights of the Child. One of the key problems is that Canada continues to have a patchwork of policies that, on the whole, have been ineffective in significantly reducing child poverty.

A Patchwork of Measures

As noted in Chapter 7, Canada does not have a unified, comprehensive, family-friendly, social democratic approach to social policies. Instead we have a tattered patchwork of policies (National Council of Welfare 2007g), which for the most part are means-tested, targeted, and seek individual-level solutions to broad social problems. For example, beyond measures committed to reducing poverty like the CCTB, in 2007 the federal government created the Working Income Tax Benefit (WITB) to supplement the earnings of the working poor. For single parents and couples, the maximum WITB rose from $1,044 in 2008 to $1,680 in 2009, and the net family income levels above which eligibility for WITB ends rose from $21,576 in 2008 to $25,700 in 2009 (Battle and Torjman 2009). While the WITB results in more money in the pockets of working-poor families, it effectively subsidizes corporate Canada and big business by allowing them to continue to pay workers inadequate wages in unstable work environments. An effective poverty-reduction strategy should include national standards on minimum wages, which would result in cost savings and increased income tax revenue.

Taking the individual-level approach, the federal government has also tried to reduce poverty among single-parent families by introducing a series of federal–provincial child support payment enforcement measures. Unacceptably high levels of non-compliance with child support orders—high default rates, particularly on the part of non-custodial fathers—throughout the 1990s lead to the creation of Bill C-41, an Act to Amend the Divorce Act, the Family Orders and Agreements Enforcement Assistance Act, and the Garnishment, Attachment and Pension Diversion Act (1997). These amendments to the Divorce Act outlined the Federal Child Support Guidelines—a simplified series of tables specifying the amount of child support to be paid by the non-custodial parent based on the payer's income (Department of Justice 2006).[6] This federal enforcement legislation was also designed to support the efforts of various new provincial enforcement agencies created to help locate spouses in breach of support orders and agreements. As part of these efforts, the new legislation gives provincial enforcement agencies access to federal sources of information (Revenue Canada data, for example) to allow the garnishment of funds from income tax refunds, Employment Insurance benefits, old age security payments, GST credits, etc., to satisfy support orders that are in default.[7] It also included a new Licence Denial Scheme that permits the denial of certain licence applications (such as a passport, pilot and air traffic controller certificates, and other federal licences) in cases of persistent default on child support (Douglas 2001). While default on child support is an important issue to be resolved, less than half of all child support cases are registered with a maintenance enforcement program (Robinson 2006); and this remains a punitive, individual-level "solution" to child poverty, that continues to be highly ineffective (Howe and Covell 2003).

These punitive, individual-level, means-tested, and targeted approaches have proven to be ineffective in combating poverty for a number of reasons. Even some of the most seemingly benevolent, individual-level, and targeted programs have been found to be problematic, including some charitable school- and community-based nutrition program aimed at feeding hungry children. For example, Raine, McIntyre, and Dayle found that while some children who were hungry were being fed through these programs, only a minority of the population being targeted (children living in poverty) was being reached. This failure to reach children who are poor could be partly attributed to parental resistance to these programs for fear of stigmatization. The researchers noted that while charitable programmes believed they provided a solution to child hunger, some programs were actually alienating and stigmatizing children living in poverty. Raine, McIntyre, and Dayle also found that charitable models often keep the causes of hunger out of public debate by drawing attention away from the underlying causes of poverty. Furthermore, the treatment of child hunger as charity depoliticizes poverty and treats poverty as something other than a social justice issue. It does little to reduce dependency on charity and reduce social inequality (Raine, McIntyre, and Dayle 2003). According to Torjman, a robust poverty strategy involves "a combination of safety net elements that help offset the impact of low income, and springboard components that create opportunities for success over the longer term" (Torjman 2008, 2). Policies and programs should protect Canadians from becoming poor, should help reduce injustice, and work towards reducing dependency and stigma. Universal programs have been especially effective in doing this, while targeted programs have not. Let us consider some examples of both successes and failures when it comes to poverty reduction from diverse provinces across Canada.

Provincial Failures

While the federal government was working on improvements to the child benefits system, it was also in the process of abolishing the Canada Assistance Plan and introducing the Canada Health and Social Transfer (see Chapter 6), which effectively reduced federal transfers for social assistance and gave new powers to the provinces. In response to this, some provinces introduced new "welfare-to-work" strategies, which restricted eligibility for social assistance, reduced benefit levels, and required an increasing number of social assistance recipients to find jobs or participate in employment-related programs (Breitkreuz 2005; Williamson and Salkie 2005).

Welfare recipients who were deemed employable, including many single mothers, would receive government benefits only after they demonstrated that they were taking steps towards gainful employment through participation in employability programs, attending school, or actively looking for work. Cuts to welfare rates and welfare-to-work programs sprang up in 1993 and 1994 in Alberta, and spread throughout other provinces and territories soon after that. Over the past decade, Ontario cut welfare rates by 21.6 percent (Raphael 2007).

In Ontario, after 1997, single mothers with children four years or older were expected to be involved in workfare activities or paid work and could be cut off all welfare payments if they do not comply.[8] Other provincial welfare programs were even more severe. Welfare programs in Saskatchewan and Alberta considered a mother to be "employable" when her youngest child was six months old; and British Columbia's welfare program stated that an applicant must prove two years' prior work experience before she or he can be eligible for welfare (Little forthcoming).

Despite low levels of welfare fraud, every province also placed great emphasis on fraud control by introducing welfare fraud hotlines. This contributed to heightened stigma, social exclusion, and higher poverty rates.

Women, and especially mothers, have been disproportionately affected by cuts to social services and recent government downsizing (Bezanson 2006; McDaniel 2002).[9] Most of these retraining and wage supplement programs specifically designed for poor single mothers did not lead to employment (Little forthcoming). In addition to the difficulty of finding employment, many mothers also realized that they would not be able to meet their child care and other employment-related expenses once the supplement to the poorly paid jobs that were part of welfare-to-work or workfare ended. Consequently, these programs did very little to remove single mothers from poverty (Little forthcoming).

Children have not benefited from the welfare reforms of the 1990s either. Williamson and Salkie (2005) found that the school readiness of children in poverty did not improve at all after the introduction of welfare reforms.

While many of these programs reduced the number of people on "welfare rolls" due to strict new eligibility and compliance rules, they were not effective in reducing poverty. Some provinces acknowledged this. For example, some ten years after the introduction of neo-liberal welfare reforms in Ontario, things seem to be changing. In 2007 the provincial Liberal party announced their commitment to poverty reduction, including efforts to reduce poverty by 25 percent in 5 years.[10] This commitment follows in the footsteps of Quebec and Newfoundland and Labrador governments, which have both implemented anti-poverty strategies.

Poverty reduction lessons from Eastern Canada

For the last ten years, Quebec has been revealing components of a family policy unparalleled in North America, aimed at reconciling work and family, promoting gender equity, and reducing family poverty (Albanese forthcoming; Roy and Bernier 2007). At the 1996 Summit on the Economy and Employment, the province's premier announced a significant shift in family policies. The 1997 White Paper argued for policy coherence and integration across domains—across social assistance, early childhood education, and employment. Its goals were to ensure fairness by offering universal support to families, providing more assistance to low-income families, facilitating the balance of work with parenting, and fostering child development and equal opportunity (Albanese forthcoming; Jenson 2001b; Paquet n.d.). In 1997, as a cornerstone of the new family policy, Quebec introduced $5/day child care for four-year-olds using child care at least three days a week, regardless of a family's income and employment status (Albanese 2006; Government of Quebec 2003). It has been argued that high-quality, affordable child care is one way out of poverty (Esping-Andersen 2007; Friendly and Prentice 2009; McCartney et al. 2007; Pascal 2009; Prentice 2007).

Quebec also developed a unified anti-poverty strategy that was initiated by a broadly based citizens' movement (National Council of Welfare 2007g; Noël 2002). The collective, made up of 30 provincial organizations and 15 regional groups, was formed in 1998 to hold public consultations and to propose social reform. This initiative resulted in the unanimous adoption by the provincial legislature in 2002 of Bill 112—the Act to Combat Poverty and Social Exclusion—a plan aimed at cutting poverty in half by 2012 (Government of Quebec 2004). With very specific initiatives and accountability structures built in, Quebec aims to have one of the lowest levels of poverty among industrialized political jurisdictions by 2013. Campaign 2000's 2007 Report Card on Child and Family Poverty in Canada documents some of its successes towards that goal.

Quebec was Canada's first province to embark on an official anti-poverty strategy (Torjman 2008). In 2005, Newfoundland and Labrador announced its own commitment to a comprehensive poverty-reduction plan, as did Nova Scotia and Ontario in 2007.[1] It is now time for Canada as a whole to develop a multi-pronged, comprehensive national poverty-reduction strategy.

Calling for a Multi-Pronged, Comprehensive, Workable National Poverty-Reduction Strategy for Canada

Many organizations, community groups, and individuals have recognized that child poverty is a serious and complex problem in this country and have committed time and resources to increasing public attention and education on the issue, as well as making governments and business more accountable.

Many organizations, including the Canadian Teachers' Federation, Food Banks Canada, the Children's Hospital of Eastern Ontario, Ontario's 25 in 5 Network, and hundreds of other community-based organizations across the country, have been stressing the need to build strong neighbourhoods, help newcomers to fulfill their potential, make housing more affordable, provide livable incomes, create employment and retraining opportunities, and increase investments in infrastructure to help reduce poverty (Canadian Teachers' Federation 2008; Food Banks Canada 2009a, 2009b; MacDonnell, Embuldeniya, and Ratanshi 2004). Attention also needs to be placed on improving adults' access to and position in the labour force (Wiegers 2002), which would inevitably require the creation of a national, accessible, affordable child-care program (McCartney et al. 2007; Penn 2004; Prentice 2007). In other words, as echoed time and again, a comprehensive, national poverty-reduction strategy is necessary for Canada.

Food Banks Canada, a national organization that represents the food bank community across Canada, for example, has recommended that the federal government take specific steps to reduce hunger in Canada by implementing a federal poverty-reduction strategy with measurable targets and timelines, which would include the following:

> increasing the value of the Working Income Tax Benefit, and widening eligibility of the program to include all households with earned incomes below the most recent low-income cut-off (LICO)
> increasing the value of the Canada Child Tax Benefit to $5,000 per child, per year
> implementing the recent recommendations of the Standing Senate Committee on Agriculture and Forestry with regard to
a) increased funding for rural housing improvement and repair
b) a review of rural housing programs to ensure they are effectively meeting objectives

Sourace: Food Banks Canada 2009a; 2009b

Citing a number of sources, the Canadian Teachers' Federation (2008), has argued for a two-pronged approach to remedy the negative relationship between poverty and school outcomes. The two prongs are (1) school-based policies such as inclusive curriculum, reduced class size, improved staffing, professional development, more school resource personnel, improved school budgets, and broader community connections to coordinate recreation and social service delivery; and (2) broader social and economic policies such as universal child care, investment in social housing, improved health care, increased minimum wages, and labour market protection and fairness. They explain that one set of reforms without the other is insufficient. Implementing these reforms together, school-based reforms and broader social and economic reforms, would go a long way towards levelling the playing field for early learners.

The National Council of Welfare (2007g, 17–18), like many other organizations, has identified a way forward for Canada, which calls for the following:

> ❯ a national anti-poverty strategy with a long-term vision and measurable targets and timelines;
> ❯ a plan of action and budget that coordinates initiatives within and across governments and other partners;
> ❯ a government accountability structure for ensuring results and for consulting Canadians in the design, implementation, and evaluation of the actions that will affect them;
> ❯ a set of agreed poverty indicators that will be used to plan, monitor, change, and assess progress.

As noted above, as part of a concrete multi-pronged approach, many have stated that a comprehensive poverty-reduction strategy should include employment support (including increased minimum wages), income replacement such as EI and other income (supplementation) support; affordable housing; early childhood education, development, and care; education, literacy, and training programs; disability income; and local social community supports (Torjman 2008). To reiterate, a robust poverty-reduction strategy should involve "a combination of safety net elements that help offset the impact of low income, and springboard components that create opportunities for success over the longer term" (Torjman 2008, 2). This would include a combination of immediate measures to help those currently in need and progressive, longer-term measures to prevent poverty, by addressing its structural, root causes (National Council of Welfare 2007g).

Preventing poverty

Children are poor because their parent or parents are poor. Therefore, one of the best approaches to combating poverty is to prevent poverty in the first place—through strengthening and supporting a parent's or parents' ties to the labour force or providing other income support where employment is not possible—including disability income.

Employment supports

Some of Canada's children who are poor are increasingly likely to be living in families where one or both parents are working, but the family income is not enough to make ends meet. This has a great deal to do with the changing nature of Canada's economy. Reviewing the trends identified in past chapters, we see that poverty rates have a great deal to do with a parent's or parents' access to the labour force, the wages they receive, and they type of jobs they hold.

Numerous sources, including Statistics Canada, have documented the rise of insecure, temporary, and part-time employment characterized by poor job quality, low wages, and no health or pension benefits. The federal and provincial governments need to work on increasing the availability of good jobs at living wages by raising minimum wages, and providing better protection through Employment Insurance (Freiler, Rothman, and Barata 2004).

Employment Insurance reforms

There is a growing consensus among Canadians that the Employment Insurance system needs reforming, with some of its earlier initiatives restored or revisited. For example, the Canadian Labour Congress has recommended the creation of uniform entrance requirements of about 360 hours, to replace both variable entrance requirements that exist across the provinces, and the 600 hours required for receiving special benefits like maternity and parental benefits (Battle and Torjman 2009).

The Canadian Labour Congress and a number of social policy think tanks have also recommended that the earnings replacement rate for EI be raised from current 55 percent to 60 percent of insurable earnings, and on the best 12 weeks of earnings (not the current 26 weeks of actual earnings). They recommend extending the maximum duration of benefits up to 50 weeks and eliminating the two-week waiting period (Battle and Torjman 2009). Overall, there is a widespread call for unifying and levelling the qualifying rules and duration of benefits and boosting the program's earnings-replacement level.

Lifelong education and training or retraining: From early childhood and beyond

A cornerstone of Canada's poverty-reduction strategy should involve the building of a universally accessible system of high-quality early childhood education and care that will support child development, early learning, and a parent's or parents' attachment to work and school (Freiler, Rothman, and Barata 2004; Friendly and Prentice 2009; Pascal 2009).

As noted in Chapter 3, children who grow up poor are at a disproportionately higher risk of dropping out of school and consequently becoming adults who are poor. High-quality early learning programs can help compensate for difficult home and community environments, and improve school success longer-term (Pascal 2009). They also allow parents to upgrade their own skills, or pursue post-secondary education and training or retraining.

Parents with more skills and post-secondary education and training are more likely to find jobs that earn higher wages (in the so-called knowledge economy) and are more resilient and less vulnerable to economic fluctuations. Governments and communities need to make provisions for ongoing upgrading, due to changing educational and skill requirements. Efforts should be made to recognize international credentials and improve collaboration between employers, occupational regulatory bodies, post-secondary institutions, community organizations, and all levels of government (Torjman 2008).

A national housing strategy

Stable, affordable, and high-quality housing is essential for the physical and emotional well-being of Canadians (Torjman 2008). However, many Canadians find themselves in poor quality, unstable housing situations (Canada Mortgage and Housing Corporation 2003a). In fact, a large portion of Canadians are likely not aware of how poorly Canada compares to other industrialized nations when it comes to housing and housing policy.

In 2007 a *Toronto Star* editorial article reported that "Canada is the only major country in the world without a national housing strategy." The *Toronto Star* warned that "until the federal government commits to devising one with the provinces, living conditions for Canadians will continue to deteriorate and despair and hardship will grow" (*Toronto Star* 2008).

In 2008 the federal government announced its intent to allocate more funds for housing and homelessness, but it needs to follow-up on its commitment (Torjman 2008), as well as work with the other levels of governments to develop a national housing strategy to address the acute shortage of affordable housing in urban, semi-rural, rural, and remote communities across Canada.

Moving out of poverty: A radically reformed social welfare system

Welfare is the social safety net of "last resort" in Canada. It aims to meet the very basic needs of individuals and families who have exhausted all other means of financial support. Across Canada, there are 13 different welfare systems—one in each province and territory—each with its own complex rules surrounding eligibility, rates of assistance, the amounts of other income recipients are allowed to have or keep, and the way applicants or recipients may question decisions regarding their cases (National Council of Welfare 2008b).

According to the National Council of Welfare, "qualifying for welfare is a complicated, cumbersome, and stigmatizing process" (2008b, 8). They add that due to the very low asset exemption rules and thresholds, applicants typically have to spend their last dollar before they can qualify for assistance. Ensuring that applicants are destitute when entering the system may result in trapping them in a "web of dependency" and actually making the exit from welfare very difficult. Beyond this, welfare rates remain extremely low across the country, with most welfare rates well below Canada's low-income cut-off (LICO), leaving many on social assistance receiving only a fraction of the basic necessities of life (National Council of Welfare 2008b). Welfare incomes for some family types in some jurisdictions have actually deteriorated in recent years.

The National Council of Welfare (2008b) has stated that governments must seriously examine the cost of providing too little, as it prevents the possibility of being hired or being productive in any larger sense, prevents people from effectively helping themselves, from pursuing longer-term training, and from moving out of poverty. It also strangles any hope for autonomy and dignity. They and many others suggest that social assistance rates should be increased, that welfare recipients receive the federal National Child Benefit Supplement where it has been clawed back by provincial governments, and that families on social assistance be consulted when making policies and considering approaches to poverty reduction.[12] At the same time, they join others in a call for a comprehensive pan-Canadian strategy to reduce poverty. This strategy consists of an action plan, targets, a timeline, accountability, and measurable indicators, and also includes a social welfare system that is integrated into a larger social and economic framework with links to child care, health, education, and labour market policies, and various services for Canadians with special and multiple needs (National Council of Welfare 2008b).

Conclusion

Canadian politicians have been well aware of the "problem" of child poverty and our poor international showing for a long time—at least since 1989 when they made a commitment to abolish it by the year 2000. It got worse before it got better. Two decades later, we are seeing some improvements, but Canada remains among one of the worst of the rich countries in regard to abolishing child poverty.

As outlined throughout this book, child poverty is a complex issue that has multiple causes and serious effects. As a result, reducing poverty will need to include a range of efforts from a variety of sources and players including employers, unions, and all levels of government, as well as community and citizens' groups. A model for this already exists in Quebec. We need to create a national anti-poverty strategy and develop a coordinated plan of action aimed at preventing poverty and helping those currently in need. This would involve raising the minimum wage rates, improving housing and social assistance, creating a national early learning and child-care system, developing and implementing family-friendly workplace practices, and pursuing the economic and social development of disadvantaged communities and neighbourhoods. At present, Canada (except Quebec, and more recently, Newfoundland and Labrador) lags behind many other developed nations on all these initiatives, calling into question its right to be considered "the envy of the world." It is time for the creation and implementation of a comprehensive national plan of action. We owe it to Canada's children.

Notes

Introduction

[1]Canada's life expectancy was high at 79.1 years; adult literacy rates were 99 percent in Canada; and standard of living was US $23,582 GDP per capita in 2000 (CBC News 2000).

[2]Those receiving disability income support make up the third largest group of food bank clients in the last five years (Food Banks Canada 2009a).

[3]Primary income source of assisted households, March 2008: Social Assistance, 50.8 percent; Employment, 14.5 percent; Disability, 12.7 percent; Pension, 6.5 percent; No Income, 5.2 percent; Other, 4.9 percent; Employment Insurance, 4.8 percent; Student Loan, 1.1 percent (Food Banks Canada 2009a).

[4]Seniors accounted for 5.7 percent of food bank clients in a typical month in 2008 (Food Banks Canada 2009a).

Chapter 1

[1]Gini coefficients have also been used in international comparisons of poverty. A Gini coefficient is a measure of inequality of incomes and wealth found in a population. It is a statistical measure of dispersion, assessing how "spread out" incomes and wealth are; measuring the gap between the most and least wealthy/highest and lowest incomes in a population. It is presented as a ratio, with values between 0 (perfect equality) and 1 (total inequality); where a low Gini coefficient indicates more equal income or wealth distribution, and a high Gini coefficient indicates more unequal

distribution. Across the globe, Gini coefficients range from a low of about 0.230 in Sweden to a high of just over 0.70 in Namibia. In 2005 the Gini coefficient for after-tax income in Canada was 0.39 (*The Gazette* 2008).

Chapter 2

[1]Since 1991 over 120 organizations and groups from across Canada have joined forces with the goal of building awareness, educating the public, and shaping public policy on child poverty. This group has called itself Campaign 2000. Its name reflects its goal of building Canadian awareness and support for the 1989 all-party House of Commons resolution to end child poverty in Canada by the year 2000. To help do this, since 2000 this organization has used official Canadian statistics and resources, in the form of annual Report Cards, to document and measure the progress towards the goal of eliminating child poverty. Copies of these report cards are widely available, very readable and reliable (citing Statistics Canada data and studies), and provide a good source of information on child poverty rates and trends in Canada today.

[2]Canada Mortgage and Housing Corporation (CMHC) was established as a government-owned corporation in 1946 to address Canada's post-war housing shortage. Since then, the agency has grown into a major national institution and Canada's premier provider of mortgage loan insurance, mortgage-backed securities, housing policy and programs, and housing research. See http://www.cmhc-schl.gc.ca/en/.

[3]Statistics Canada warns that the numbers for PEI, Alberta, Nova Scotia, Newfoundland, New Brunswick, and Manitoba should be "used with caution" due to small sample size.

[4]It is important to note that single-parenthood does not inevitably lead to poverty, as is the case in some Scandinavian countries with more social democratic social policies.

[5]The rate for non-Aboriginal people in 2006 was 81.6 percent, up from 80.3 percent in 2001 (Statistics Canada 2009a).

[6]LSIC is a three-wave, longitudinal study of immigrants (2001–2005) that surveys newcomers at 6, 24, and 48 months after their arrival to Canada. It identifies their admission class and difficulties they encounter with settlement issues (housing, employment, income, etc.).

[7]About 80 percent of Ontario's immigrant and visible minorities live in the GTA. Children of non-European heritage made up close to 50 percent of the GTA's children and about 70 percent of the GTA's

children living in poverty (Children's Aid Society of Toronto 2008).
Toronto has the most challenging housing market in the country
with above-average rents and housing prices. In Vancouver, rents
are cheaper than in Toronto, but housing prices are higher (CMHC
2009).

[8]Among the large cities most often chosen by immigrants, Montreal
has the most affordable housing market. However, the immigrant
population there has the least ability to pay for housing, given their
low labour force participation rates (CMHC 2009, 3).

[9]Note that this was even before the dramatic job losses that made
headlines starting in fall 2008.

Chapter 3

[1]"Hungry families" were 6 times more likely to be headed by single
mothers; over 8 times more likely to be receiving social assistance
or welfare; 4 times more likely to be of Aboriginal descent; and 54
percent of "hungry households" received their main income from
employment (McIntyre, Walsh, and Connor 2001).

[2]The rate of diabetes is three to five times that of the general population
(Assembly of First Nations 2007b).

[3]Howe and Covell (2003) note that poverty is associated with a higher
incidence of child maltreatment, often due to everyday stressors
including parental feelings of anxiety, frustration, anger associated
with unemployment or underemployment, overcrowded housing,
lack of various supports, and insufficient resources.

[4]Maternal responsiveness has been found to be related to regular
reading to children, as it is associated with vocabulary development.
(Senechal and LeFevre 2002).

Chapter 4

[1]For related research on Saskatoon, Saskatchewan, see Peters and
McCreary 2008. For related research on London, Ontario, see
Mead 2008.

Chapter 6

[1]These were not without problems. See Little Forthcoming.

[2]The problem remains that there are many Canadians earning wages
considered to be above minimum wage but still having a difficult
time making ends meet. These people are considered to be low-
wage workers, or those who Statistics Canada measures to work
full-time but earn less than $375 per week. Between 1980 and
2004, the proportion of adult employees who were considered

low-wage workers changed very little, hovering at about 16 percent over that entire period (Morissette and Picot 2005).

Chapter 7

[1] The Organization for Economic Co-operation and Development states that it "brings together the governments of countries committed to democracy and the market economy from around the world to: support sustainable economic growth; boost employment; raise living standards; maintain financial stability; assist other countries' economic development; contribute to growth in world trade." It "provides a setting where governments compare policy experiences, seek answers to common problems, identify good practice and coordinate domestic and international policies" (see www.oecd.org). As of 2005, 30 countries were members of the OECD.

[2] In 2007 Canada ranked 15 out of 24 countries compared. This was the result of improvements in Australia's rate and some deterioration in other countries, rather than improvements in Canada, as Canada's rate remained about the same (UNICEF 2007).

[3] Since 1999, but especially since 2005, the UK has embarked on comprehensive package of reforms and a national poverty reduction strategy aimed at significantly reducing child poverty. While it has not met all targets, child poverty rates have been declining (Collin 2007b).

[4] According to Chen and Corak (2008), in no OECD country compared were demographic characteristics as a whole a force implying higher child poverty rates; rather changes in labour markets and government were the major causes of changes in child poverty.

[5] Some have argued for a paradigm shift that goes beyond a "family responsibility" model (programs for children that assume parents are responsible for all decisions) to an "investing in children" paradigm (programs that assume parents have responsibility for children but (governments, community groups, etc., in partnership are also important (Jenson 2004a; Beauvais and Jenson 2001).

Chapter 8

[1] Prior to 1989 national security reform initiatives were put in place through a 1973 joint federal–provincial review of the Canadian social security system. This special initiative resulted in, among other things, two proposals: an income support program for those not in the labour force and an income supplement program for low-income families with children. After the inability to achieve

national consensus across provinces, the federal government unilaterally proceeded with the implantation of the Refundable Child Tax Credit, which included a reduction in the Family Allowance and targeted benefits to low-income families (Warriner and Peach 2007).

[2]The Government of Quebec agreed with the basic principles of the NCB but chose not to participate because it wanted to assume control over income support for children in that province (Government of Canada 2007).

[3]Some provinces claw back all or part of the NCB Supplement from their child benefit program. Recognizing the negative impact of this federal–provincial agreement for families on social assistance, in 2004 the Manitoba government ended the claw back of the NCB Supplement, putting almost $14 million each year back into the pockets of low-income Manitoba families (Government of Manitoba 2007).

[4]Maximum payments for the first child rose from $1,520 in July 1996 to $3,416 in July 2009. The Caledon Institute of Social Policy and other groups have suggested a maximum $5,000 CCTB as the target for a mature child benefit that reduces poverty and helps parents (Battle and Torjman 2009).

[5]Some have argued that part of the problem in implementing the UN Convention on the Rights of the Child in general, and poverty reduction measures in particular, is related to Canada's political organization. Canada is a federation of provinces and territories—13 separate jurisdictions—whereby the federal government is responsible for the development and maintenance of the national body through its control of foreign policy, defence, citizenship and immigration, currency, trade and commerce, criminal law, and the administration of the lives of Canada's First Nations who are governed and recognized by the Indian Act. Since Confederation, the provinces, have retained control of the preservation of regional differences and the functioning of everyday life through their control of education, social services, health care, labour regulations, and standards (e.g., minimum wage), language rights, and the regular administration of the criminal justice system. While there have been efforts to maintain universal, cross-Canada standards (such as in health care), this has amounted to a patchwork of policies and practices across the country which make studying something like "childhood in Canada" very difficult and implementing Canada-wide reforms virtually impossible. These jurisdictional complexities have been

identified as part of the problem when implementing policies and programs aimed at assisting children and in the fulfilling of Canada's international obligations.

[6]The Federal Child Support Guidelines were amended in 2006. Amendments include updated Federal Child Support Tables to reflect changes to provincial, territorial, and federal tax rates (Department of Justice 2006).

[7]Default refers to no payments, partial payments, late payments, and late partial payments of child support.

[8]Prior to welfare reforms, lone mothers in all provinces could provide full-time care to their children and receive social assistance until their youngest child was at least school age and in some provinces, until their youngest was 18 years old (Williamson and Salkie 2005).

[9]In the face of significant cut-backs in available public resources and services, low-income mothers have been found to rely on private resources through a wide range of activities, including providing for themselves, small-scale entrepreneurial activities, exchanges of goods and services, and careful managing of scarce resources (Collins, Neysmith, Porter, and Reitsma-Street 2009).

[10]See Ontario's 25 in 5 Network for Poverty Reductio (www.25in5. ca) for details.

[11]The Manitoba government has also been working to reduce poverty. For details see Government of Manitoba 2007. For more on Newfoundland and Labrador's poverty reduction plan, see http://www.hrle.gov.nl.ca/hrle/poverty/index.html, Collin 2007a, and Community Development Halton 2007.

[12]For a detailed breakdown of recommendations, including details of the Temporary Income Program, see Battle and Torjman 2009.

Further Reading

Introduction

Albanese, P. 2009. *Children in Canada Today*. Toronto: Oxford University Press.

Canada Mortgage and Housing Corporation (CMHC). 2003. Family Homelessness: Causes and Solutions. *Research Highlight*. Socio-economic Series 03-006. Ottawa: Canada Housing and Mortgage Corporation.

Food Banks Canada. 2009a. HungerCounts. 2008. Toronto: Food Banks Canada. http://foodbankscanada.ca/documents/HungerCount_en_fin.pdf.

Ontario Association of Food Banks. 2008. A Gathering Storm: The Price of Food, Gasoline, and Energy and Changing Economic Conditions in Ontario. Toronto: Ontario Association of Food Banks.

UNICEF. 1990a. Convention on the Rights of the Child. New York: United Nations.

———. 1990b. World Summit for Children. New York: United Nations. http://www.unicef.org/wsc.

Chapter 1

Campaign 2000. 2002. UN Special Session on Children: Putting Promises into Action, A Report on a Decade of Child and Family Poverty in Canada. Toronto: Campaign 2000. http://www.campaign2000.ca/rc/unsscMAY02/MAY02statusreport.pdf.

Campaign 2000. 2007. 2007 Report Card on Child and Family Poverty in Canada: It Takes a Nation to Raise a Generation, Time for a National Poverty Reduction Strategy. Toronto: Campaign 2000. http://www.campaign2000.ca/rc/rc07/2007_C2000_National ReportCard.pdf.

Government of Canada. 1997 (and amendments). National Children's Agenda. http://www.socialunion.ca/nca/June21-2000/english/index_e.html.

Government of Canada. 2002. A Canada Fit for Children. http://www.hrsdc.gc.ca/en/cs/sp/sdc/socpol/publications/2002-002483/canadafite.pdf.

Mendelson, M. 2005. Measuring Child Benefits, Measuring Child Poverty. Ottawa: Caledon Institute of Social Policy. http://www.caledoninst.org/Publications/PDF/525ENG%2Epdf.

National Council of Welfare. 2008. Factsheet 1: Poverty Lines 2007. Ottawa: National Council of Welfare. http://www.ncwcnbes.net/documents/researchpublications/OtherFactSheets/PovertyLines/2007ENG.pdf.

Phipps, S., and L. Curtis. 2000. Poverty and Child Well-Being in Canada and the United States: Does it Matter How we Measure Poverty? Working Paper Series, Applied Research Branch of Strategic Policy. SP-556-01-03E. Gatineau: Human Resources Development Canada.

Wiegers, W. 2002. The Framing of Poverty as "Child Poverty" and Its Implications for Women. Ottawa: Status of Women Canada.

Chapter 2

Beiser, M., F. Hou, I. Hyman, and M. Tousignant. 2002. Poverty, Family Process and the Mental Health of Immigrant Children in Canada. *American Journal of Public Health* 92 (2): 220–27.

Campaign 2000. 2008. Family Security in Insecure Times: 2008 Report Card on Child and Family Poverty in Canada. Toronto: Campaign 2000. http://www.campaign2000.ca/rc/C2000%20Report%20Card%20FINAL%20Nov%2010th08.pdf.

Canada Mortgage and Housing Corporation (CMHC). 2009. Settling In: Newcomers in the Canadian Housing Market, 2001–2005. *Research Highlights*. Socio-economic Series 09-002. Ottawa: Canada Mortgage and Housing Corporation.

Children's Aid Society of Toronto. 2008. Greater Trouble in Greater Toronto: Child Poverty in the GTA. Toronto: Children's Aid Society of Toronto.

Kazemipur, A., and S. Halli. 2001. The Changing Colour of Poverty in Canada. *Canadian Review of Sociology and Anthropology* 38 (2): 217–38.

Little, M.H. 1998. *No Car, No Radio, No Liquor Permit: The Moral Regulation of Single Mothers in Ontario*. Toronto: Oxford University Press.

MacDonnell, S. 2007. Losing Ground: The Persistent Growth of Poverty in Canada's Largest City. Toronto: United Way of Greater Toronto. http://www.uwgt.org/whoWeHelp/reports/pdf/LosingGround-fullReport.pdf.

Picot, G., F. Hou, and S. Coulombe. 2007. Chronic Low Income and Low-Income Dynamics among Recent Immigrants. Business and Labour Market Analysis. Cat. no. 11F0019MIE, No. 294. Ottawa: Statistics Canada.

Trocmé, N., D. Knoke, and C. Blackstock. 2004. Pathways to the Overrepresentation of Aboriginal Children in Canada's Child Welfare System. *Social Service Review* 78 (4): 577–600.

United Way of Greater Toronto. 2004. Poverty by Postal Code. Toronto: United Way of Greater Toronto.

Chapter 3

Blau, D.M. 1999. The Effect of Income on Child Development. *Review of Economics and Statistics* 81 (2): 261–76.

Bradshaw, J. 2002. Child Poverty and Child Outcomes. *Children and Society* 16: 131–40.

Burdette, H.L., and R.C. Whitaker. 2005. A National Study of Neighborhood Safety, Outdoor Play, Television Viewing and Obesity in Preschool Children. *Pediatrics* 116 (3): 657–62.

Chung, H., and C. Muntaner. 2006. Political and Welfare State Determinants of Infant and Child Health Indicators: An Analysis of Wealthy Countries. *Social Science and Medicine* 63 (3): 829–42.

McLoyd, V.C. 1998. Socioeconomic Disadvantage and Child Development. *American Psychologist* 53: 185–204.

Messer, L., L. Vinikoor, B. Laraia, J. Kaufman, J. Eyster, C. Holzman, J. Culhane, I. Elo, J. Burke, and P. O'Campo. 2008. Socioeconomic Domains and Associations with Preterm Birth. *Social Science and Medicine* 67 (8): 1247–57.

National Institute of Child Health and Human Development Early Child Care Research Network. 2005. Duration and Developmental Timing of Poverty and Children's Cognitive and Social Development from Birth through Third Grade. *Child Development* 76 (4): 795–810.

Nikièma, B., M. Zunzunegui, L. Séguin, L. Gauvin, and L. Potvin. 2008. Poverty and Cumulative Hospitalization in Infancy and Early Childhood in the Quebec Birth Cohort: A Puzzling Pattern of Association. *Maternal and Child Health Journal* 12 (4): 534–44.

Phipps, S., and L. Lethbridge. 2006. *Income and the Outcomes of Children*. Ottawa: Statistics Canada, Analytical Studies Branch Research Paper Series. http://www.statcan.ca/english/research/ 11F0019MIE/11F0019MIE2006281.pdf.

Ricciuto, L., and V. Tarasuk. 2007. An Examination of Income-Related Disparities in the Nutritional Quality of Food Selections among Canadian Households from 1986–2001. *Social Science and Medicine* 64 (1): 186–98.

Ross, D., and P. Roberts. 1999. *Income and Child Well-Being: A New Perspective on the Poverty Debate*. Ottawa: Canadian Council on Social Development. http://www.ccsd.ca/pubs/inckids/index.htm.

Séguin, L., X.Q. Xu, L. Potvin, M.-V. Zunzunegui, and K. Frohlich. 2003. Effects of Low Income on Infant Health. *Canadian Medical Association Journal* 168 (12): 1533–38.

Urquia, M., J. Frank, R. Glazier, and R. Moineddin. 2007. Birth Outcomes by Neighbourhood Income and Recent Immigration in Toronto. *Health Reports* 18 (4): 1–10.

Yeung, J., M. Linver, and J. Brooks-Gunn. 2002. How Money Matters for Young Children's Development: Parental Investment and Family Processes. *Child Development* 73 (6): 1861–79.

Chapter 4

Ball, K., A. Timperio, and D. Crawford. 2009. Neighbourhood Socioeconomic Inequalities in Food Access and Affordability. *Health and Place* 15 (2): 578–85.

Bauserman, R. 2002. Child Adjustment in Joint-Custody Versus Sole-Custody Arrangements: A Meta-Analytic Review. *Journal of Family Psychology* 16 (1): 91–102.

Canada Mortgage and Housing Corporation (CMHC). 2003 (revised 2006). Housing Quality and Children's Socioemotional Health. *Research Highlights*. Socio-economic Series 03-021. Ottawa: Canada Mortgage and Housing Corporation.

Caughy, M.O., S.M. Nettles, and P. O'Campo. 2008. The Effects of Residential Neighbourhood on Child Behavior Problems in First Grade. *American Journal of Community Psychology* 42: 39–50.

Department of Justice. 2006. *Federal Child Support Guidelines: Step-by-Step*. Ottawa: Minister of Justice and the Attorney General of Canada. http://www.justice.gc.ca/en/ps/sup/pub/guide/guide.pdf.

Peters, E., and T. McCreary. 2008. Poor Neighbourhoods and the Changing Geography of Food Retailing in Saskatoon, Saskatchewan, 1984–2004. *Canadian Journal of Urban Research* 17 (1): 78–106.

Power, A. 2007. *City Survivors: Bringing up Children in Disadvantaged Neighbourhoods*. Bristol: Polity Press.

Strohschein, L. 2005. Parental Divorce and Child Mental Health Trajectories. *Journal of Marriage and Family* 67 (5): 1286–1300.

Chapter 5

Hughes, K., and G. Lowe. 2000. Surveying the "Post-industrial" Landscape: Information Technologies and Labour Market Polarization in Canada. *Canadian Review of Sociology and Anthropology* 37 (1): 29–53.

Morissette, R., and Y. Ostrovsky. 2005. The Instability of Family Earnings and Family Income in Canada, 1986 to 1991 and 1996 to 2001. Cat. no. 11F0019MIE; No. 265. Analytical Studies Branch Research Paper Series. Ottawa: Statistics Canada.

Roy, F. 2006. From She to She: Changing Patterns of Women in the Canadian Labour Force. *Canadian Economic Observer* 3.1–3.10.

Sauvé, R. The Current State of Canadian Family Finances, 2008 Report. Family Finances Series. Ottawa: Vanier Institute of the Family. http://www.vifamily.ca/library/cft/famfin08.pdf.

Silver, S., J. Shields, and S. Wilson. 2005. Restructuring of Full-Time Workers: A Case of Transitional Dislocation or Social Exclusion in Canada? Lessons from the 1990s. *Social Policy and Administration* 39 (7): 786–801.

Statistics Canada. 2006. *The Wealth of Canadians: Overview of the Results of the Survey of Financial Security*. Cat. no. 13F0026MIE; No. 001. Ottawa: Statistics Canada.

Statistics Canada. 2009a. *The Canadian Labour Market at a Glance, 2007*. Cat. no. 71-222-X. Ottawa: Statistics Canada.

Chapter 6

Battle, K. 2009. Gender Aspects of Employment Insurance, 3. Ottawa: Caledon Institute of Social Policy.

Mahon, R. 2006. Of Scalar Hierarchies and Welfare Redesign: Childcare in Three Canadian Cities. *Transactions of the Institute of British Geographers* 31 (4): 452–66.

National Council of Welfare. 2008. *Welfare incomes, 2006 and 2007*. Cat. no. HS51-1/2007E. Ottawa: Her Majesty the Queen in Right of Canada/National Council of Welfare.

Raphael, D. 2007. *Poverty and Policy in Canada*. Toronto: Canadian Scholars' Press.

Sigle-Rushton, W., and J. Waldfogel. 2007. The Incomes of Families with Children: A Cross-National Comparison. *Journal of European Social Policy* 17 (4): 299–318.

Smeeding, T. 2005. *Poor People in Rich Nations*. Syracuse: Syracuse University.

Statistics Canada. 2005. Fact Sheet on Minimum Wage. *Perspectives on Labour* 18–23.

Statistics Canada. 2009a. Minimum Wage. *Perspectives on Labour and Income*, 1–6. Ottawa: Statistics Canada.

Warriner, W., and I. Peach. 2007. *Canadian Social Policy Renewal, 1994–2000*. Halifax: Fernwood.

Chapter 7

Collin, C. 2007. Poverty Reduction Strategies in the United Kingdom and Ireland. PRB 07-28E. Ottawa: Parliamentary Information and Research Service. Political and Social Affairs Division.

Corak, M., C. Lietz, and H. Sutherland. 2005. The Impact of Tax and Transfer Systems on Children in the European Union. Innocenti Working Paper 2005–04. Florence: UNICEF Innocenti Research Centre.

Heyman, J., M. Barrera, and A. Earle. 2008. The Working Poor: Canada and the World. *Policy Options* 29 (8): 47–52.

Kamerman, S., M. Neuman, J. Waldfogel, and J. Brooks-Gunn. 2003. Social Policies, Family Types and Child Outcomes in Selected OECD Countries. OECD Social, Employment and Migration Working Papers, No. 6. Paris: OECD Directorate For Employment, Labour and Social Affairs.

National Council of Welfare. 2007. *Solving Poverty: Four Cornerstones of Workable National Strategy for Canada*. Ottawa: National Council of Welfare. http://www.ncwcnbes.net/documents/researchpublications/ResearchProjects/NationalAntiPovertyStrategy/2007Report-SolvingPoverty/ReportENG.pdf.

UNICEF. 2005. *Report Card 6 – Child Poverty in Rich Countries, 2005*. Florence: UNICEF Innocenti Research Centre. http://unicef.gr/reports/rc06/UNICEF%20CHILD%20POVERTY%20IN%20RICH%20COUNTRIES%202005.pdf.

UNICEF. 2007. *Report Card 7 – Child Poverty in Perspective: An ovErview of Child Well-Being in Rich Countries*. Florence: UNICEF Innocenti Research Centre.

Warriner, W., and I. Peach. 2007. *Canadian Social Policy Renewal, 1994–2000.* Halifax: Fernwood.

Whiteford, P., and W. Adema. 2007. What Works Best in Reducing Child Poverty: A Benefit or Work Strategy? OECD Social, Employment and Migration Working Paper. No. 51. Paris: OECD Directorate For Employment, Labour and Social Affairs.

Chapter 8

Andreychuk, R., and J. Fraser. 2007. *Children: The Silenced Citizens: Effective Implementation of Canada's International Obligations with Respect to the Rights of Children.* Final Report of the Standing Senate Committee on Human Rights. Ottawa: Senate Committees Directorate. http://www.parl.gc.ca/39/1/parlbus/commbus/senate/com-e/huma-e/rep-e/rep10apr07-e.htm; http://www.fncfcs.com/docs/Children_TheSilentCitizens_April2007.pdf.

Battle, K. 2008. *Bigger and Better Child Benefit: A $5,000 Canada Child Tax Benefit.* Ottawa: Caledon Institute of Social Policy.

Battle, K., and S. Torjman. 2009. The Federal Role in Poverty Reduction. Ottawa: Caledon Institute of Social Policy. http://www.caledoninst.org/Publications/PDF/766ENG.pdf.

Collin, C. 2007. Poverty Reduction Strategies in Quebec and Newfoundland and Labrador. Parliamentary Information and Research Service, Political and Social Affairs Division: Library of Parliament. PRB 07-23E. http://www.parl.gc.ca/information/library/PRBpubs/prb0723-e.pdf.

Community Development Halton. 2007. Poverty Reduction Strategies in Quebec and Newfoundland and Labrador. *Community Dispatch* 12 (3): 1–6.

Freiler, C., L. Rothman, and P. Barata. 2004. Pathways to Progress: Structural Solutions to Address Child Poverty. Toronto: Campaign 2000 (Policy Perspectives).

Government of Canada. 2008. *The National Child Benefit-Progress Report 2006.* Ottawa: Government of Canada. http://www.nationalchildbenefit.ca/eng/pdf/ncb_progress_report_2006.pdf.

Government of Manitoba. 2007. Reducing Poverty in Manitoba – Budget 2007. Budget Paper E. Winnipeg: Government of Manitoba.

National Council of Welfare. 2007. *Solving Poverty: Four Cornerstones of a Workable National Strategy for Canada,* vol. 126. Ottawa: National Council of Welfare. http://www.ncwcnbes.net/documents/researchpublications/ResearchProjects/NationalAntiPovertyStrategy/2007Report-SolvingPoverty/ReportENG.pdf.

Noël, A. 2002. *A Law against Poverty: Quebec's New Approach to Combating Poverty and Social Exclusion*. Ottawa: Canadian Policy Research Networks.

Penn, H. 2004. *Child Care and Early Childhood Development Programmes and Policies: The Relationship to Eradicating Child Poverty*. London: Childhood Poverty Research and Policy Centre.

Torjman, S. 2008. *Poverty Policy*. Ottawa: Caledon Institute of Social Policy.

References

Akyeampong, E. Canada's Unemployment Mosaic, 2000 to 2006. *Perspectives* 20 (2): 5–12. Statistics Canada Cat. no. 75-001XIE.

Albanese, P. 2006. Small Town, Big Benefits: The Ripple Effect of $7/Day Child Care. *Canadian Review of Sociology and Anthropology* 43 (2): 125–40.

———. 2009a. $7/Day, $7/Hour, 7 Days a Week: Juggling Commutes, Shift Work and Childcare in a Changing ("New") Economy. In *Women Across Borders*, ed. J. Klaehn. 26–40. Toronto: Black Rose Books.

———. 2009b. *Children in Canada Today*. Toronto: Oxford University Press.

———. Forthcoming. Balancing Paid Work and Family Responsibilities: Lessons on Family Policy from Quebec. In *The Family/Paid Work Contradiction: Challenges and Possibilities*, eds. C. Krull and J. Sempruch. Vancouver: University of British Columbia Press.

Andreychuk, R., and J. Fraser. 2007. *Children: The Silenced Citizens. Effective Implementation of Canada's International Obligations with Respect to the Rights of Children*. Final Report of the Standing Senate Committee on Human Rights. Ottawa: Senate Committees Directorate. http://www.parl.gc.ca/39/1/parlbus/commbus/senate/com-e/huma-e/rep-e/rep10apr07-e.htm; http://www.fncfcs.com/docs/Children_TheSilentCitizens_April2007.pdf.

Amato, P., and J. Zuo. 1992. Rural Poverty, Urban Poverty, and Psychological Well-Being. *Sociology Quarterly* 33 (2): 229–40.

Armstrong, R. 2000. Mapping the Conditions of First Nations Communities. *Canadian Social Trends* 3: 28–32. Toronto: Thompson Educational.

Assembly of First Nations. 2007a. The $9 Billion Myth Exposed: Why First Nations Poverty Endures. http://www.afn.ca/cmslib/general/M-Ex.pdf.

Assembly of First Nations. 2007b. State of Diabetes among First Nations Peoples. http://www.afn.ca/article.asp?id=3604.

August, M. 2008. Social Mix and Canadian Public Housing Redevelopment: Experiences in Toronto. *Canadian Journal of Urban Research* 17 (1): 82–100.

Ball, K., A. Timperio, and D. Crawford. 2009. Neighbourhood Socioeconomic Inequalities in Food Access and Affordability. *Health and Place* 15(2): 578–85.

Battle, K. 2007. Child Poverty: The Evolution and Impact of Child Benefits. In *A Question of Commitment: Children's Rights in Canada*, eds. R.B. Howe and K. Covell. 21–44. Waterloo: Wilfrid Laurier University Press.

———. 2008. *Bigger and Better Child Benefit: A $5,000 Canada Child Tax Benefit*. Ottawa: Caledon Institute of Social Policy.

———. 2009. *Gender Aspects of Employment Insurance, 3*. Ottawa: Caledon Institute of Social Policy.

Battle, K., and S. Torjman. 2009. *The Federal Role in Poverty Reduction*. Ottawa: Caledon Institute of Social Policy. http://www.caledoninst.org/Publications/PDF/766ENG.pdf.

Bauserman, R. 2002. Child Adjustment in Joint-Custody Versus Sole-Custody Arrangements: A Meta-Analytic Review. *Journal of Family Psychology* 16 (1): 91–102.

Beauvais, C., and J. Jenson. 2001. *Two Policy Paradigms: Family Responsibility and Investing in Children*. Ottawa: Canadian Policy Research Networks.

Beiser, M., A. Shik, and M. Curyk. 1999. *New Canadian Children and Youth Study: Literature Review*. Ottawa: Health Canada.

Beiser, M., F. Hou, V. Kaspar, and S. Noh. 2000. *Changes in Poverty Status and Developmental Behaviours: A Comparison of Immigrant and Non-Immigrant Children in Canada*. Ottawa: Human Resources Development Canada, Applied Research Branch Strategic Policy. http://www.hrsdc.gc.ca/en/cs/sp/sdc/pkrf/publications/research/2000-001332/2000-001332.pdf.

Beiser, M., F. Hou, I. Hyman, and M. Tousignant. 2002. Poverty, Family Process and the Mental Health of Immigrant Children in Canada. *American Journal of Public Health* 92 (2): 220–27.

Béland, D., and J. Myles. 2004. Special Issue on Social Policy: Canadian International Perspectives—Introduction. *Canadian Journal of Sociology* 29 (2): 165–68.

Berry, B. 2007. Disparities in Free Time Activity in the United States: Trends and Explanations. *Sociological Perspectives* 50 (2): 177–208.

Bezanson, K. 2006. *Gender, the State, and Social Reproduction: Household Insecurity in Neo-Liberal Times.* Toronto: University of Toronto Press.

Blackstock, C., T. Cross, J. George, I. Brown, and J. Formsma. 2006. *Reconciliation in Child Welfare: Touchstones of Hope for Indigenous Children, Youth and Families.* Ottawa: Centre of Excellence for Child Welfare and National Indian Child Welfare Association. http://www.reconciliationmovement.org/docs/Touchstones_of_Hope.pdf.

Blau, D.M. 1999. The Effect of Income on Child Development. *Review of Economics and Statistics* 81 (2): 261–76.

Bourdieu, P., and J.C. Passeron. 1977. *Reproduction in Education, Culture and Society.* Beverley Hills: Sage Press.

Bradshaw, J. 2002. Child Poverty and Child Outcomes. *Children and Society* 16: 131–40.

Breitkreuz, R. 2005. Engendering Citizenship? A Critical Feminist Analysis of Canadian Welfare-to-Work Policies and the Employment Experiences of Lone Mothers. *Journal of Sociology and Social Welfare* 32 (2): 147–165.

Brighton, Richard. 2008. Millions of UK young in poverty. BBC News, September 30. http://news.bbc.co.uk/2/hi/uk_news/2641734.stm.

Brooks, S., and L. Miljan. 2003. *Public Policy in Canada.* Toronto: Oxford University Press.

Brooks-Gunn, J., and G.J. Duncan. 1997. The Effects of Poverty on Children. In *Children and Poverty: The Future of Children*, vol. 7, 55–71, ed. R.E. Behrman. Los Altos, CA: Centre for Future of Children, David and Lucile Packard Foundation.

Brooks-Gunn, J., and L. Markham. 2005. The Contribution of Parenting to Ethnic and Racial Gaps in School Readiness. *Future of Children* 15 (1): 139–68. http://www.futureofchildren.org/information2826/information_show.htm?doc_id=255990.

Brotchie, K. 2006. Poverty in Thunder Bay: A Statistical Reference. Phase 2, 20. Thunder Bay: Thunder Bay Economic Justic Committee.

Burdette, H.L., and R.C. Whitaker. 2005. A National Study of Neighborhood Safety, Outdoor Play, Television Viewing and Obesity in Preschool Children. *Pediatrics* 116 (3): 657–62.

Campaign 2000. 2000. Child Poverty in Canada Report Card 2000. Toronto: Campaign 2000. http://www.campaign2000.ca/rc/00/index.html.

————. 2002. UN Special Session on Children: Putting Promises into Action, A Report on a Decade of Child and Family Poverty in Canada. Toronto: Campaign 2000. http://www.campaign2000.ca/rc/unssc MAY02/MAY02statusreport.pdf.

————. 2007. 2007 Report Card on Child and Family Poverty in Canada: It Takes a Nation to Raise a Generation, Time for a National Poverty Reduction Strategy. Toronto: Campaign 2000. http://www.campaign2000.ca/rc/rc07/2007_C2000_National ReportCard.pdf.

————. 2008. Family Security in Insecure Times: 2008 Report Card on Child and Family Poverty in Canada. Toronto: Campaign 2000. http://www.campaign2000.ca/rc/C2000%20Report%20Card%20 FINAL%20Nov%2010th08.pdf.

Canada Mortgage and Housing Corporation (CMHC). 2001 (revised 2006). Children and Youth in Homeless Families: Shelter Spaces and Services. *Research Highlights*. Socio-economic Series 80. Ottawa: Canada Mortgage and Housing Corporation. http://www.cmhc-schl.gc.ca/odpub/pdf/62492.pdf.

————.2003a. Family Homelessness: Causes and Solutions. *Research Highlight*. Socio-economic Series 03-006. Ottawa: Canada Mortgage and Housing Corporation.

————. 2003b (revised 2006). Housing Quality and Children's Socioemotional Health. *Research Highlights*. Socio-economic Series: 03-021. Ottawa: Canada Mortgage and Housing Corporation.

————. 2009. Settling In: Newcomers in the Canadian Housing Market, 2001–2005. *Research Highlights*. Socioeconomic Series 09-002. Ottawa: Canada Mortgage and Housiing Corporation.

Canada Online. 2009. Minimum Wage in Canada. http://canadaonline.about.com/library/bl/blminwage.htm

Canadian Teachers' Federation. 2008. Child Poverty and Schools: CTF Brief Presented to the Senate Committee on Social Affairs, Science and Technology. http://www.ctf-fce.ca/e/publications/brief/Brief_on_Child_ poverty%20_Senate_Committee.pdf.

Canadian Broadcasting Corporation News (CBC News). 2000. Canada #1 in UN Survey—Again. Cbc.ca, November 10. http://www.cbc.ca/world/story/2000/06/29/UN_report000629.html.

————. 2009. Recession, 15,000 job losses forecast: Alberta finance minister. CBC News.ca, February 19. http://www.cbc.ca/canada/edmonton/story/2009/02/19/edm-alberta-economy.html.

Caughy, M.O., S.M. Nettles, and P. O'Campo. 2008. The Effects of Residential Neighbourhood on Child Behavior Problems in First Grade. *American Journal of Community Psychology* 42: 39–50.

Chen, W.-H., and M. Corak. 2008. Child Poverty and Changes in Child Poverty. *Demography* 45 (3): 537–553.

Children's Aid Society of Toronto. 2008. Greater Trouble in Greater Toronto: Child Poverty in the GTA. Toronto: Children's Aid Society of Toronto.

Chung, H., and C. Muntaner. 2006. Political and Welfare State Determinants of Infant and Child Health Indicators: An Analysis of Wealthy Countries. *Social Science and Medicine* 63 (3): 829–42.

Citizenship and Immigration Canada. 2005. *Recent Immigrants in Metropolitan Areas*. Ottawa: Citizenship and Immigration. http://www.cic.gc.ca/english/pdf/research-stats/2001-canada.pdf.

Collin, C. 2007a. Poverty Reduction Strategies in Quebec and Newfoundland and Labrador. Ottawa Parliamentary Information and Research Service, Political and Social Affairs Division: Library of Parliament. PRB 07-23E. http://www.parl.gc.ca/information/library/PRBpubs/prb0723-e.pdf.

——— 2007b. Poverty Reduction Strategies in the United Kingdom and Ireland. PRB 07-28E. Ottawa: Parliamentary Information and Research Service, Political and Social Affairs Division.

Collins, S.B., S. Neysmith, E. Porter, and M. Reitsma-Street. 2009. Women's Provisioning Work: Counting the Cost for Women Living in Low Income. *Community, Work and Family* 12 (1): 21–37.

Community Development Halton. 2007. Poverty Reduction Strategies in Quebec and Newfoundland and Labrador. *Community Dispatch* 12 (3): 1–6.

Corak, M. 2006. Principles and Practices for Measuring Child Poverty. *International Social Security Review* 59 (2): 3–35.

Corak, M., C. Lietz, and H. Sutherland. 2005. The Impact of Tax and Transfer Systems on Children in the European Union. Innocenti Working Paper 2005–04. Florence: UNICEF Innocenti Research Centre.

Corak, M., and W. Pyper. 1995. *Workers, Firms and Unemployment Insurance*. Cat. no. 73-505-XPE. Ottawa: Statistics Canada.

Crockett, E.G., K.L. Clancy, and J. Bowering. 1992. Comparing the Cost of a Thrifty Food Plan Market Basket in Three Areas of New York State. *Journal of Nutrition Education* 24: 71–78.

Dean, H., and E. Sellers. 2007. Comorbidities and Microvascular Complications of Type 2 Diabetes in Children and Adolescents. *Pediatric Diabetes* (Supplement 9) 8: 35–41.

Dennison, B., T.A. Erb, and P.L. Jenkins. 2002. Television Viewing and Television in Bedroom Associated with Overweight Risk Among Low-Income Preschool Children. *Pediatrics* 109 (6): 1028–35.

Department of Justice. 2002. *Children Come First: A Report to Parliament Reviewing the Provisions and Operation of the Federal Child Support Guidelines*, 2 vols. Ottawa: Minister of Justice and Attorney General of Canada.

———. 2006. *Federal Child Support Guidelines: Step-By-Step*. Ottawa: Minister of Justice and the Attorney General of Canada. http://www.justice.gc.ca/en/ps/sup/pub/guide/guide.pdf.

Douglas, K. 2001. *Divorce Law in Canada*. Ottawa: Law and Government Division, Government of Canada.

Dunn, J., H. Cheng, T. O'Connor, and L. Bridges. 2004. Children's Perspectives on their Relationships with their Nonresident Fathers: Influences, Outcomes and Implications. *Journal of Child Psychology and Psychiatry* 45 (3): 553–66.

Esping-Andersen, G. 1990. *The Three Worlds of Welfare Capitalism*. Princeton, NJ: Princeton University Press.

———. 2007. Sociological Explanations of Changing Income Distributions. *American Behavioral Scientist* 50 (5): 639–58.

First Call: BC Child & Youth Advocacy Coalition. 2009. Citing BC Campaign 2000 Child Poverty Report Card 2008; UNICEF Child Poverty in Rich Countries 2005; Standing Committee on Health 2007. *Increased Economic Inequality, Facts*. http://www.firstcallbc.org/economicEquality-facts.html.

Food Banks Canada. 2009a. *Hunger Counts, 2008*. Toronto: Food Banks Canada. http://foodbankscanada.ca/documents/HungerCount_en_fin.pdf.

———. 2009b. *About Hunger in Canada*. Toronto: Food Banks Canada. http://foodbankscanada.ca/main2.cfm?id=10718629-B6A7-8AA0-6D9B9CE378DE06DA.

Fortier, S. 2006. On Being a Poor Child in America: Views of Poverty from 7–12-Year-Olds. *Journal of Children and Poverty* 12 (2): 113–28.

Freiler, C., and J. Cerny. 1998. *Benefiting Canada's Children: Perspectives on Gender and Social Responsibility*. Ottawa: Status of Women Canada.

Freiler, C., L. Rothman, and P. Barata. 2004. Pathways to Progress: Structural Solutions to Address Child Poverty. Toronto: Campaign 2000 (Policy Perspectives).

Friendly, M., and S. Prentice. 2009. *About Canada: Child Care*. Halifax: Fernwood.

Galarneau, D. 2005. Earnings of Temporary versus Permanent

Employees. *Perspectives* 6 (1): 5–18. Statistics Canada Cat. no. 75-001-XIE.

Gassman-Pines, A., and H. Yoshikawa. 2006. The Effects of Antipoverty Programs on Children's Cumulative Level of Poverty-Related Risk. *Developmental Psychology* 42 (6): 981–99.

Gennetian, L., and C. Miller. 2002. Children and Welfare Reform: A View from an Experimental Welfare Program in Minnesota. *Child Development* 73 (2): 601–21.

Gera, S., and K. Mang. 1998. The Knowledge-based Economy: Shifts in Industrial Output. *Canadian Public Policy* 24.2: 149–84.

Government of Canada. 1997 (and amendments). *National Children's Agenda*. Ottawa: Government of Canada. http://www.socialunion.ca/nca/June21-2000/english/index_e. html.

——— 2002. *A Canada Fit for Children*. Ottawa: Government of Canada. http://www.hrsdc.gc.ca/en/cs/sp/sdc/socpol/publications/2002-002483/canadafite.pdf.

———. 2007. *The National Child Benefit—Progress Report 2005*. Ottawa: Government of Canada. Cat. no. HS1-3/2005E. http://www.nationalchildbenefit.ca.

———. 2008. *The National Child Benefit-Progress Report 2006*. Ottawa: Government of Canada. http://www.nationalchildbenefit.ca/eng/pdf/ncb_progress_report_2006.pdf.

Government of Manitoba. 2007. Reducing Poverty in Manitoba—Budget 2007. (Budget Paper E). Winnipeg: Government of Manitoba.

Government of Quebec. 2003. *Development and Funding Scenarios to Ensure the Permanence, Accessibility and Quality of Childcare Services: Consultations 2003*. Quebec: Ministère de l'Emploi et de la Solidarité sociale.

———. 2004. *Reconciling Freedom and Social Justice: A Challenge for the Future—Government Action Plan to Combat Poverty and Social Exclusion*. Quebec: Ministère de l'Emploi et de la Solidarité sociale. http://www.mess.gouv.qc.ca/publications/index_en.asp?categorie=portail|cr|saca|sr|SRport|jeunes&type=MG#liste.

Harvey, D., and M. Reed. 1996. The Culture of Poverty: An Ideological Analysis. *Sociological Perspectives* 39 (4): 465–95.

Healthy Child Manitoba. 2003. *A New Generation of Canadian Families: Raising Young Children – A New Look at Data from National Surveys*. Ottawa: Human Resources Development Canada. http://www.gov.mb.ca/healthychild/ecd/raising_young_children.pdf.

Hertz, R. 2006. *Single by Chance, Mothers by Choice: How Women are Choosing Parenthood without Marriage and Creating the New American Family*. New York: Oxford University Press.

Heymann, J., M. Barrera, and A. Earle. 2008. The Working Poor: Canada and the World. *Policy Options* 29 (8): 47–52.

Horowitz, C.R., K.A. Colson, P.L. Herbert, and K. Lancaster. 2004. Barriers to Buying Healthy Foods for People with Diabetes: Evidence of Environmental Disparities. *American Journal of Public Health* 94 (9): 1549–54.

Howe, R.B., and K. Covell. 2003. Child Poverty in Canada and the Rights of the Child. *Human Rights Quarterly* 25(4): 1067–87.

———, eds. 2007. *A Question of Commitment: Children's Rights in Canada.* Waterloo: Wilfrid Laurier University Press.

Hughes, K. and G. Lowe. 2000. Surveying the "Post-industrial" Landscape: Information Technologies and Labour Market Polarization in Canada. *Canadian Review of Sociology and Anthropology* 37 (1): 29–53.

Interfaith Social Assistance Reform Coalition. 1998. *Our Neighbours' Voices: Will We Listen?* Toronto: James Lorimer.

Jenson, J. 2001a. Canada's Shifting Citizenship Regime: Investing in Children. In *The Dynamics of Decentralization: Canadian Federalism and British Devaluation*, eds. T. Salmon and M. Keating. 107–23. Montreal: McGill-Queen's University Press.

———. 2001b. Family Policy, Child Care and Social Solidarity: The Case of Quebec. In *Changing Child Care: Five Decades of Child Care Advocacy and Policy in Canada*, ed. S. Prentice. 39–62. Halifax: Fernwood.

———. 2004a. Changing the Paradigm: Family Responsibility or Investing in Children. *Canadian Journal of Sociology* 29 (2): 169–192.

———. 2004b. Family Responsibility or Investing in Children: Shifting the Paradigm. *Canadian Journal of Sociology* 29 (2): 169–192.

Jones, C., L. Clark, J. Grusec, R. Hart, G. Plickert, and L. Tepperman. 2002. *Poverty, Social Capital, Parenting and Child Outcomes in Canada.* Ottawa: Human Resources Development Canada, Working Paper Series of the Applied Research Branch of Strategic Policy.

Juby, H., C. Le Bourdais, and N. Marcil-Gratton. 2005. Sharing Roles, Sharing Custody? Couples' Characteristics and Children's Living Arrangements at Separation. *Journal of Marriage and Family* 67: 157–72.

Kamerman, S., M. Neuman, J. Waldfogel, and J. Brooks-Gunn. 2003. Social Policies, Family Types and Child Outcomes in Selected OECD Countries. OECD Social, Employment and Migration Working Papers, No. 6. Paris: OECD Directorate For Employment, Labour and Social Affairs.

Kazemipur, A. and S. Sitall Halli. 2000. Neighbourhood Poverty in Canadian Cities. *Canadian Journal of Sociology* 25 (3): 369–381.

———. 2001. The Changing Colour of Poverty in Canada. *Canadian Review of Sociology and Anthropology* 38 (2): 217–38.

Kerr, D. 2004. Family Transformations and the Well-being of Children: Recent Evidence from Canadian Longitudinal Data. *Journal of Comparative Family Studies* 35 (10): 73–90.

Kerr, D., and R. Beaujot. 2002. Family Relations, Low Income and Child Outcomes: A Comparison of Canadian Children in Intact-, Step-, and Lone-Parent Families. *International Journal of Comparative Sociology* 43 (2): 134–52.

———. 2003. Child Poverty and Family Structure in Canada, 1981–1997. *Journal of Comparative Family Studies* 34 (3): 321–35.

Kirkpatrick, S., and V. Tarasuk. 2003. The Relationship Between Low Income and Household Food Expenditure Patterns in Canada. *Public Health Nutrition* 6 (6): 589–97.

Krahn, H. and G. Lowe. 2002. *Work, Industry and Canadian Society.* Toronto: Thomson.

Kufeldt, K. 2002. Sharing the Care of our Children in Changing Societal Context. *Child and Family Social Work* 7: 131–39.

Kusserow, A. 2004. *American Individualism: Child Rearing and Social Class in Three Neighborhoods.* New York: St. Martin's Press.

Lareau, A. 2000. Social Class And The Daily Lives Of Children: A Study From The United States. *Childhood* 7 (2): 155–71.

———. 2003. *Unequal Childhoods: Class, Race and Family Life.* Berkeley: University of California Press.

Lewis, M.K., and A.J. Hill. 1998. Food Advertising on British Children's Television: A Content Analysis and Experimental Study with Nine-Year-Olds. *International Journal of Obesity* 22: 206–14.

Lewis, O. 1964. The Culture of Poverty, 149–173. In *Explosive Forces in Latin America*, eds. J.J. TePaske and S. Nettleson Fisher. Columbus: Ohio State University Press.

———. 1966. *La Vida: A Puerto Rican Family in the Culture of Poverty: San Juan and New York.* New York: Random House.

———. 1968. The Culture of Poverty, 187–200. In *On Understanding Poverty, Perspectives from the Social Sciences*, ed. D.P. Moynihan. New York: Basic Books.

Little, M.H. 1998. *No Car, No Radio, No Liquor Permit: The Moral Regulation of Single Others in Ontario.* Toronto: Oxford University Press.

———. Forthcoming. The Increasing Invisibility of Mothering. In *Demystifying the Family/Work Contradiction: Challenges and*

Possibilities, eds. C. Krull and J. Sempruch. Vancouver: UBC Press.

Little, M.H., and I. Morrison. 1999. "Pecker Detectors are Back": Regulation of the Family Form in Ontario Welfare Policy. *Journal of Canadian Studies* 34 (2): 110–36.

Lowe, G. 2000. *The Quality of Work: A People-Centred Agenda*. Toronto: Oxford University Press.

McCartney, K., E. Dearing, B. Taylor, and K. Bub. 2007. Quality Child Care Supports the Achievement of Low-Income Children: Direct and Indirect Pathways Through Caregiving and Home Environment. *Journal of Applied Developmental Psychology* 28 (5, 6): 411–26.

McDaniel, S. 2002. Women's Changing Relations to the State and Citizenship: Caring and Intergenerational Relations in Globalizing Western Democracies. *Canadian Review of Sociology and Anthropology* 39 (2): 125–50.

MacDonnell, S. 2007. *Losing Ground: The Persistent Growth of Poverty in Canada's Largest City*. Toronto: United Way of Greater Toronto. http://www.uwgt.org/whoWeHelp/reports/pdf/LosingGround-fullReport.pdf.

MacDonnell, S., D. Embuldeniya, and F. Ratanshi. 2004. *Poverty by Postal Code: The Geography of Neighbourhood Poverty, City of Toronto, 1981–2001*. Toronto: United Way of Greater Toronto.

McIntyre, L., G. Walsh, and S. Connor. 2001. A Follow-up Study of Child Hunger in Canada: June 2001. Cat. no. SP-443-06-01E W-01-1-2E. Ottawa: Applied Research Branch Strategic Policy. Human Resources Development Canada. http://www.hrsdc.gc.ca/eng/cs/sp/sdc/pkrf/publications/research/2001-000172/SP-443-06-01E.pdf.

McLoyd, V.C. 1998. Socioeconomic Disadvantage and Child Development. *American Psychologist* 53: 185–204.

Mahon, R. 2006. Of Scalar Hierarchies and Welfare Redesign: Childcare in Three Canadian Cities. *Transactions of the Institute of British Geographer* 31 (4): 452–66.

Marcil-Gratton, N., and C. Le Bourdais. 1999. *Custody, Access and Child Support: Findings from the National Longitudinal Survey of Children and Youth*. CSR 1999-3E. Ottawa: Department of Justice.

Mead, N. 2008. The Sprawl of Food Deserts. *Environmental Health Perspectives* 116 (8): A335.

Mendelson, M. 2005. Measuring Child Benefits, Measuring Child Poverty. Ottawa: Caledon Institute of Social Policy. http://www.caledoninst.org/Publications/PDF/525ENG%2Epdf.

Menzies, H. 2000. Umbilical Cords and Digital Fibre-Optics:

Communication and the Disembodiments of Digital Globalization. *Gazette* 62 (3, 4): 271–80.

Messer, L.; L. Vinikoor, B. Laraia, J. Kaufman, J. Eyster, C. Holzman, J. Culhane, I. Elo, J. Burke, and P. O'Campo. 2008. Socioeconomic Domains and Associations with Preterm Birth. *Social Science and Medicine* 67 (8): 1247–57.

The Gazette. 2008. Lies, Damn Lies – and Statistics Canada. *Canada.com*, May 3. http://www2.canada.com/montrealgazette/news/editorial/story.html?id=e284e4a3-7ff1-43b2-b76b-d6e3badd11f6.

Morissette, R., and G. Picot. 2005. *Low-Paid Work and Economically Vulnerable Families over the Last Two Decades.* Cat. no. 11F0019; No. 248. Ottawa: Statistics Canada.

Morissette, R., and Y. Ostrovsky. 2005. The Instability of Family Earnings and Family Income in Canada, 1986 to 1991 and 1996 to 2001. Cat. no. 11F0019MIE; No. 265. Analytical Studies Branch Research Paper Series. Ottawa: Statistics Canada.

Morrissette, R., X. Zhang, and M. Drolet. 2002. Are Families Getting Richer? *Canadian Social Trends* 66: 15–19.

Myles, J. 1988. The Expanding Middle: Some Canadian Evidence on the Deskilling Debate. *The Canadian Review of Sociology and Anthropology* 25 (3): 335–64.

Nair, H., and A. Murray. 2005. Predictors of Attachment Security in Preschool Children from Intact and Divorced Families. *The Journal of Genetic Psychology* 166 (3): 245–63.

National Council of Welfare. 2004. Market Basket Measure. Ottawa: National Council of Welfare. http://www.ncwcnbes.net/documents/researchpublications/OtherPublications/2004Report-IncomeForLiving/Factsheets/mbm ENG.pdf.

———. 2007a. Income: Aboriginal Children and Youth in Need. First Nations, Metis, and Inuit Children and Youth, 28. Ottawa: National Council of Welfare.

———. 2007b. Poverty Statistics 2004: Poverty by Age and Sex, 2004.Ottawa: National Council of Welfare. http://www.ncwcnbes.net/documents/researchpublications/ResearchProjects/PovertyProfile/2004/PovertyRates-ByAgeSex ENG.pdf.

———. 2007c. Poverty Statistics 2004: Poverty Rates by Number and Age Group of Children, 2004. Ottawa: National Council of Welfare. http://www.ncwcnbes.net/documents/researchpublications/ResearchProjects/PovertyProfile/2004/Children-AgesENG.pdf.

———. 2007d. Fact Sheet: Definitions of The Most Common Poverty Lines Used in Canada, June 2003. Ottawa: National Council of

Canada. http://www.ncwcnbes.net/documents/researchpublications/OtherFactSheets/PovertyLines/2003 DefinitionsPovertyLinesENG.htm.

———. 2007e. Poverty Statistics 2004: Average Depth of Poverty in Dollars, by Family Type, 2004. Ottawa: National Council of Welfare. http://www.ncwcnbes.net/documents/researchpublications/ResearchProjects/Poverty Profile/2004/DepthPoverty-DollarsENG.pdf.

———. 2007f. Poverty Statistics 2004: Poverty Trends, All Persons, 1980–2004. Ottawa: National Council of Welfare. http://www.ncwcnbes.net/documents/research publications/ResearchProjects/PovertyProfile/2004/PovertyRates-TrendsENG.pdf.

———. 2007g. Solving Poverty: Four Cornerstones of Workable National Strategy for Canada. Ottawa: National Council of Welfare. http://www.ncwcnbes.net/documents/researchpublications/ResearchProjects/NationalAntiPovertyStrategy/2007Report-SolvingPoverty/ReportENG.pdf.

———. 2008a. Factsheet 1: Poverty Lines 2007. Ottawa: National Council of Welfare. http://www.ncwcnbes.net/documents/research publications/OtherFactSheets/PovertyLines/2007ENG.pdf.

———. 2008b. *Welfare Incomes, 2006 and 2007.* Cat. no. HS51-1/2007E. Ottawa: National Council of Welfare.

National Institute of Child Health and Human Development Early Child Care Research Network. 2005. Duration and Developmental Timing of Poverty and Children's Cognitive and Social Development from Birth through Third Grade. *Child Development* 76 (4): 795–810.

Nikièma, B., M. Zunzunegui, L. Séguin, L. Gauvin, and L. Potvin. 2008. Poverty and Cumulative Hospitalization in Infancy and Early Childhood in the Quebec Birth Cohort: A Puzzling Pattern of Association. *Maternal and Child Health Journal* 12 (4): 534–44.

Noël, A. 2002. *A Law Against Poverty: Quebec's New Approach to Combating Poverty and Social Exclusion.* Ottawa: Canadian Policy Research Networks.

O'Brien Caughy, M., S. Murray Nettles, and P. O'Campo. 2008. The Effect of Residential Neighborhood on Child Behavior Problems in First Grade. *American Journal of Community Psychology* 42 (1, 2): 39–50.

Olsen, L., J.L. Bottorff, P. Raina, and C.J. Frankish. 2008. An Ethnography of Low-Income Mothers' Safeguarding Efforts. *Journal of Safety Research* 39: 609–16.

Ontario Association of Food Banks. 2008. A Gathering Storm: The Price of Food, Gasoline, and Energy and Changing Economic

Conditions in Ontario. Toronto: Ontario Association of Food Banks.

Organization for Economic Co-operation and Development (OECD). 2005. *Society at a Glance: OECD Social Indicators 2005 Edition.* http://www.oecd.org/document/24/0,3343,en_2649_34637_2671576_1_1_1_1,00.html.

Palameta, B. 2004. Low Income Among Immigrants and Visible Minorities. *Perspectives* 5 (4): 12–17. Statistics Canada Cat. no. 75-001-XIE.

Paquet, N., n.d. Toward a Policy on Work-Family Balance: Discussion Paper, Abridged Edition. Quebec: Ministère de l'Emploi et de la Solidarité sociale.

Pascal, C. 2009. *With Our Best Future in Mind: Implementing Early Learning in Ontario.* Report to the Premier by the Special Advisor on Early Learning.

Penn, H. 2004. *Child Care and Early Childhood Development Programmes and Policies: The Relationship to Eradicating Child Poverty.* London: Childhood Poverty Research and Policy Centre.

Peters, E., and T. McCreary. 2008. Poor Neighbourhoods and the Changing Geography of Food Retailing in Saskatoon, Saskatchewan, 1984–2004. *Canadian Journal of Urban Research.* 17 (1): 78–106.

Phipps, S.A., P.S. Burton, L.S. Osberg, and L.N. Lethbridge. 2006. Poverty and the Extent of Child Obesity in Canada, Norway and the United States. *Obesity Reviews* 7 (1): 5–12.

Phipps, S., and L. Curtis. 2000. *Poverty and Child Well-Being in Canada and the United States: Does It Matter How We Measure Poverty?* Working Paper Series, Applied Research Branch of Strategic Policy. SP-556-01-03E. Gatineau: Human Resources Development Canada.

Phipps, S., and L. Lethbridge. 2006. *Income and the Outcomes of Children.* Ottawa: Statistics Canada, Analytical Studies Branch Research Paper Series. www.statcan.ca/english/research/11F0019MIE/11F0019MIE2006281.pdf.

Picot, G., F. Hou, and S. Coulombe. 2007. *Chronic Low Income and Low-Income Dynamics among Recent Immigrants.* Business and Labour Market Analysis. Cat. no. 11F0019MIE; No. 294. Ottawa: Statistics Canada.

Porr, C., J. Drummond, and S. Richter. 2006. Health Literacy as an Empowerment Tool for Low-income Mothers. *Family and Community Health* 29 (4): 328–35.

Power, A. 2007. *City Survivors: Bringing up Children in Disadvantaged Neighbourhoods.* Bristol: Polity Press.

Power, E. 2005. The Unfreedom of Being Other: Canadian Lone Mothers' Experiences of Poverty and "Life on the Cheque". *Sociology* 39 (4): 643–60.

Prentice, S. 2007. Less Access, Worse Quality: New Evidence about Poor Children and Regulated Child Care in Canada. *Journal of Children and Poverty* 13 (1): 57–73.

Raine, K., L. McIntyre, and J. Dayle. 2003. The Failure of Charitable School- and Community-based Nutrition Programmes to Feed Hungry Children. *Critical Public Health* 13 (2): 155–69.

Raphael, D. 2007. *Poverty and Policy in Canada.* Toronto: Canadian Scholars' Press.

Renfrew County Child Poverty Action Network (CPAN). 2008. *Ontario's Poverty Reduction Plan Consultation.* Toronto: Queen's Park.

Renfrew County Child Poverty Action Network (CPAN). 2009. About Child Poverty. www.renfrewcountycpan.ca.

Ricciuto, L., and V. Tarasuk. 2007. An Examination of Income-Related Disparities in the Nutritional Quality of Food Selections among Canadian Households from 1986–2001. *Social Science and Medicine* 64 (1): 186–98.

Roberts, D., and U. Foehr. 2004. *Kids and Media in America.* Cambridge: Cambridge University Press.

Robinson, P. 2006. *Child and Spousal Support: Maintenance Enforcement Survey Statistics, 2003/2004.* Cat. no. 85-228-XIE. Ottawa: Statistics Canada.

Robson-Haddow, J. 2004. *Key to Tackling Child Poverty: Income Support for Immediate Needs and Assets for their Future.* Ottawa: Caledon Institute of Social Policy.

Rose, D., and N. Bodor. 2006. Household Food Insecurity and Overweight Status in Young School Children: Results from the Early Childhood Longitudinal Study. *Pediatrics* 117 (2): 464–73.

Ross, D., and P. Roberts. 1999. Income and Child Well-being: A New Perspective on the Poverty Debate. Ottawa: Canadian Council on Social Development. http://www.ccsd.ca/pubs/inckids/index.htm.

Ross, D., P. Roberts, and K. Scott. 2000. Family Income and Child Well-being. *Isuma* 1, 2: 51–54.

Rotermann, M. 2007. Marital Breakdown and Subsequent Depression. *Health Reports.* 16 (2): 33–44. Ottawa: Statistics Canada.

Roy, F. 2006. From She to She: Changing Patterns of Women in the Canadian Labour Force. *Canadian Economic Observer* 3.1–3.10.

Roy, L. and Jean Bernier. 2007. *Family Policy, Social Trends and Fertility in Quebec: Experimenting with the Nordic Model?* Quebec: Ministère de la Famille, des Aînés et de la Conditio Féminine.

Royal Commission on the Status of Women. 1970. *Report on the Royal Commission on the Status of Women.* Ottawa: Information Canada.

Russell, M., B. Harris, and A. Gockel. 2008. Parenting in Poverty: Perspectives of High-Risk Parents. *Journal of Children and Poverty* 14 (1): 83–98.

Saint-Martin, D. 2002. Apprentissage social et changement institutionnel: La politique de "Investissement dans l'enfance" au Canada et en Grande-Bretagne. *Politique et sociétés* 21 (3): 41–67.

Sauvé, R. The Current State of Canadian Family Finances, 2008 report. Family Finances Series. Ottawa: Vanier Institute of the Family. http://www.vifamily.ca/library/cft/famfin08.pdf.

Scott, K. 1998. *Women and the CHST: A Profile of Women Receiving Social Assistance in 1994.* Ottawa: Status of Women Canada.

Séguin, L., X. Qian Xu, L. Potvin, M.-V. Zunzunegui, and K. Frohlich. 2003. Effects of Low Income on Infant Health. *Canadian Medical Association Journal* 168 (12): 1533–38.

Sen, A. 1999. *Development as Freedom.* New York: Random House.

Senate of Canada,. 2007. http://sen.parl.gc.ca/SenWeb/speeches/details.asp?lang=en&sen=63&speechID-573.

Senechal, M., and J. LeFevre. 2002. Parental Involvement in the Development of Children's Reading Skills: A Five Year Longitudinal Study. *Child Development* 73 (2): 445–60.

Shields, J., K. Rahi, and A. Scholtz. 2006. Voices from the Margins: Visible Minority Immigrant and Refugee Youth Experiences with Employment Exclusion in Toronto. No. 47. Working Paper Series. Toronto: CERIS/Joint Centre of Excellence for Research on Immigration and Settlement.

Sigle-Rushton, W., and J. Waldfogel. 2007. The Incomes of Families with Children: A Cross-National Comparison. *Journal of European Social Policy* 17 (4): 299–318.

Silver, S., J. Shields, and S. Wilson. 2005. Restructuring of Full-time Workers: A Case of Transitional Dislocation or Social Exclusion in Canada? Lessons from the 1990s. *Social Policy and Administration* 39 (7): 786–801.

Smeeding, T. 2005. *Poor People in Rich Nations.* Syracuse: Syracuse University.

Smith, H., and D. Ley. 2008. Even in Canada? The Multiscalar Construction and Experience of Concentrated Immigrant Poverty in Gateway Cities. *Annals of the Association of American Geographers* 98 (3): 686–713.

Smoyer-Tomic, K., J. Spence, K. Raine, C. Amrhein, N. Cameron, V. Yasenovskiy, N. Cutumisu, E. Hemphill, and J. Healy. 2008. The Association between Neighbourhood Socioeconomic Status and Exposure to Supermarkets and Fast Food Outlets. *Health and Place* 14 (4): 740–54.

Sridhar, D. 2009. Linkages between Nutrition, Ill-health and Education. Background Paper Prepared for UNESCO's Education for All Global Monitoring Report 2009: *Overcoming Inequality: Why Governance Matters.* http://unesdoc.unesco.org/images/0017/001780/178022e.pdf.

Stanwick, R. 2006. Canada Gets a Marginal Grade in Childhood Injury. *Canadian Medical Association Journal* 175 (8): 845.

Statistics Canada. 1996. Family Incomes, 1995. *The Daily.* December 11. Ottawa: Statistics Canada.

———. 2003. Aboriginal Peoples of Canada: A Demographic Profile. Cat. no. 96F0030XIE2001007. Ottawa: Statistics Canada.

———. 2004. Update on Economic Analysis. Cat. no. 11-623. XIE. Ottawa: Statistics Canada. http://www.statcan.ca/english/freepub/11-623-XIE/2003001/trdescrip.htm.

———. 2005a. Aboriginal People Living in Metropolitan Areas. *The Daily.* June 23. Ottawa: Statistics Canada.

———. 2005b. Canada's Aboriginal Population in 2017. *The Daily.* June 28. Ottawa: Statistics Canada.

———. 2005c. Fact Sheet on Minimum Wage. *Perspectives on Labour* 18–23.

———. 2006a. Income trends in Canada, 1976–2006, Table 802.

———. 2006b. The Wealth of Canadians: Overview of the Results of the Survey of Financial Security. Cat. no. 13F0026MIE; No. 001. Ottawa: Statistics Canada.

———. 2007a. Income in Canada, 2005. Cat. no. 75-202-XIE. Ottawa: Statistics Canada. http://www.statcan.ca/english/freepub/75-202-XIE/75-202-XIE2005000.pdf.

———. 2007b. Incomes of Canadians. *The Daily.* May 3. Ottawa: Statistics Canada.

———. 2007c. Women in Canada: Work Chapter Updates. Cat. no. 89F0133XIE. Ottawa: Statistics Canada.

———. 2008a. Aboriginal Peoples in Canada in 2006: Inuit, Métis and First Nations, 2006 Census: Findings. Cat. no. 97-558-XWE2006001. Ottawa: Statistics Canada.

———. 2008b. Changing Patterns in Canadian Home Ownership and Shelter Costs. *The Daily,* June 4. Ottawa: Statistics Canada.

———. 2008c. Income in Canada, 2006. Cat. no. 75-202-X. Ottawa: Statistics Canada.

———. 2008d. Spending Patterns in Canada. Cat. no. 62-202-X. Ottawa: Statistics Canada.

———. 2009a. The Canadian Labour Market at a Glance, 2007. Cat. no. 71-222-X. Ottawa: Statistics Canada.

———.2009b. Employment Insurance. *The Daily,* March 24. Ottawa: Statistics Canada.

———. 2009c. Labour Force Survey. *The Daily,* April 9. Ottawa: Statistics Canada. http://www.statcan.gc.ca/daily-quotidien/090409/dq090409a-eng.htm.

———. 2009d. Minimum Wage. *Perspectives on Labour and Income,* 1–6. Ottawa: Statistics Canada.

———. 2009e. Renfrew County and District Health Unit, 2006 Community profiles. http://www.12.statcan.gc.ca/census-recense ment/2006/dp-pd/prof/92-591/details/page.cfm?Lang=E&Geo1= 3557&Geo2=PR&Code2=35&Data=Count&SearchText=Renfrew %20COunty&SearchType=Begins&SearchPR=01&B1=All& Custom=. .

———. 2009f. Table 2: Share of Employees Working for Minimum Wage or Less, by Province. Labour Force Survey. Ottawa: Statistics Canada. http://www.statcan.gc.ca/pub/75-001-x/tables-tableaux/ topics-sujets/minimumwage-salaireminimum/2008/tbl02-eng. htm.

Strohschein, L. 2005. Parental Divorce and Child Mental Health Trajectories. *Journal of Marriage and Family* 67 (5): 1286–1300.

Thomas, E. 2006. *Readiness to Learn at School among Five-Year-Old Children in Canada.* Children and Youth Research Paper Series. Ottawa: Statistics Canada. http://www.statcan.ca/english/ research/89-599-MIE/89-599-MIE2006004.pdf.

Torjman, S. 2008. *Poverty Policy.* Ottawa: Caledon Institute of Social Policy.

Toronto Star. 2008. Canada Lacks Housing Strategy.*Thestar.com.* March 5. http://www.thestar.com/comment/article/309365.

Tough, S., D. Johnston, J. Siever, G. Jorgenson, L. Slocombe, C. Lane, and M. Clarke. 2006. Does Supplementary Prenatal Nursing and Home Visitation Support Improved Resource Use in a Universal Health Care System? A Randomized Controlled Trial in Canada. *Birth* 33 (3): 183–94.

Tremblay, S., N. Ross, and J.-M. Berthelot. 2001. Factors Affecting Grade 3 Student Performance in Ontario: A Multilevel Analysis. *Education Quarterly Review* 7 (4): 25–36. Statistics Canada Cat. no. 81-003.

Trocmé, N., D. Knoke, and C. Blackstock. 2004. Pathways to the Overrepresentation of Aboriginal Children in Canada's Child Welfare System. *Social Service Review* 78 (4): 577–600.

UNICEF. 1990a. Convention on the Rights of the Child. New York: United Nations.

———. 1990b. World Summit for Children. New York: United Nations. http://www.unicef.org/wsc/.

———. 2000. *Report Card: A League Table of Child Poverty in Rich Nations.* Issue No. 1. Florence: UNICEF Innocenti Research Centre.

———. 2005. *Report Card 6: Child Poverty in Rich Countries 2005.* Florence: UNICEF Innocenti Research Centre. http://unicef.gr/reports/rc06/UNICEF%20CHILD%20POVERTY%20IN%20RICH%20COUNTRIES%202005.pdf.

———. 2007. *Report Card 7 – Child Poverty in Perspective: An Overview of Child Well-being in Rich Countries.* Florence: UNICEF Innocenti Research Centre. http://www.unicef-irc.org/publications/article.php?type=3&id_article=49.

United Way of Greater Toronto. 2004. *Poverty by Postal Code.* Toronto: United Way of Greater Toronto.

US Department of Labor. 2008. *Comparisons of Annual Labor Force Statistics, 10 Countries, 1960-2007.* Washington. U.S. Bureau of Labor Statistics. http://www.bls.gov/fls/flscomparelf.htm.

Urquia, M., J. Frank, R. Glazier, and R. Moineddin. 2007. Birth Outcomes by Neighbourhood Income and Recent Immigration in Toronto. *Health Report* 18 (4): 1–10.

Utter, J., R. Scragg, and D. Schaff. 2006. Association between Television Viewing and Commonly Advertised Foods among New Zealand Children and Youth. *Public Health Nutrition* 9 (5): 606–12.

Vanier Institute of the Family. 2009. Becoming a "Lone-mother." *Fascinating Families* Issue 16. http://www.vifamily.ca/families/ff16.pdf.

Verdon, L. 2007. Are 5-Year-Old Children Ready to Learn at School? Family Income and Home Environment Contexts. *Education Matters* 4, 1.

Wallerstein, J., and J. Kelly. 1980. *Surviving the Breakup: How Children and Parents Cope with Divorce.* New York: Basic Books.

Warriner, W., and I. Peach. 2007. *Canadian Social Policy Renewal, 1994–2000*. Halifax: Fernwood.

Webber, M. 1998. *Measuring Low Income and Poverty in Canada: An update*. Cat. no. 98-13, 75F0002M. Ottawa: Statistics Canada.

Weininger, E., and A. Lareau. 2003. Translating Bourdieu into the American Context: The Question of Social Class and Family-School Relations. *Poetics* 31 (5, 6): 375–402.

White, M. 2003. Retraining Programs for Displaced Workers in the Post-Industrial Era: An Exploration of Government Policies and Programs in Canada and England. *Compare* (Journal of British Association for International and Comparative Education) 33 (4): 497–505.

Whiteford, P., and W. Adema. 2007. What Works Best in Reducing Child Poverty: A Benefit or Work Strategy? OECD Social, Employment and Migration Working Paper. No. 51. Paris: OECD Directorate For Employment, Labour and Social Affairs.

Whitehead, N., W. Callaghan, C. Johnson, and L. Williams. 2009. Racial, Ethnic, and Economic Disparities in the Prevalence of Pregnancy Complications. *Maternal and Child Health Journal* 13 (2): 198–205.

Wiegers, W. 2002. *The Framing of Poverty as "Child Poverty" and Its Implications for Women*. Ottawa: Status of Women Canada.

Wilkinson, R.G. 2005. *The Impact of Inequality: How to Make Sick Societies Healthier*. New York: New Press.

Williamson, D., and F. Salkie. 2005. Welfare Reforms in Canada: Implications for the Well-being of Pre-school Children in Poverty. *Journal of Children and Poverty* 11 (1): 55–76.

Wilson, W.J. 1996. *When Work Disappears: The World of the New Urban Poor*. New York: Vintage.

Yeung, J., M. Linver, and J. Brooks-Gunn. 2002. How Money Matters for Young Children's Development: Parental Investment and Family Processes. *Child Development* 73 (6): 1861–79.

Zeytinoglu, I.U., B. Seaton, W. Lillevik, and J. Moruz. 2005. Working in the Margins: Women's Experiences of Stress and Occupational Health Problems in Part-time and Casual Retail Jobs. *Women and Health* 41 (1): 87–107.

Zhang, X. 2009. Earnings of Women with and without Children. *Perspectives* 10 (3): 5–13. Statistics Canada Cat. no. 75-001-X.

Index

Every possible effort has been made to trace the original source of text and visual material contained in this book. Where the attempt has been unsuccessful, the publisher would be pleased to hear from copyright holders to rectify any errors or omissions.